Prepare to Defend Yourself...
How to Navigate the Healthcare System
& Escape with Your Life

This book's publication is supported by the
Texas A&M School of Rural Public Health, whose mission is
to improve the health of communities through education,
research, service, outreach, and creative partnerships.

PREPARE toDEFEND YOURSELF

...How to Navigate the Healthcare System & Escape with Your Life

MATTHEW MINSON, MD

TEXAS A&M UNIVERSITY PRESS • COLLEGE STATION

LIBRARY OF CONGRESS CATALOGING-IN-PUBLICATION DATA

Minson, Matthew, 1961– author.

Prepare to defend yourself ... how to navigate the healthcare system and

escape with your life / Matthew Minson, MD.

pages cm —

Includes bibliographical references and index.

ISBN 978-1-62349-115-4 (paper, with flaps : alk. paper) —

ISBN 978-1-62349-162-8 (e-book)

1. Medical care—United States—Popular works.

2. Patient participation—United States.

3. Medical personnel and patient—United States. I. Title.

RA395.A3M533 2014

610.7306'9—dc23

2013036447

For Kelli,
without whom it all
would be insufferable

CONTENTS

INTRODUCTION

CHARACTERS OF MODERN MEDICAL MYTHOLOGY: Ms. CERBERUS

THE THREE HEADED CLERK AT THE GATES OF HEALTHCARE

W hat follows is 100 percent true. I have changed the names, but the names are important, because the experience, sadly, is too common. You can call what I experienced by any number of names: sudden enlightenment, an epiphany, a moment of clarity . . . a metaphoric two-by-four to the side of the head.

It all started with a lump. A small lump behind my ear that I could feel and that had over the span of a month increased in size. It's important that I explain that I am a physician, because I can be considered—if nothing else—an insider when it comes to the healthcare system. Yet it was this experience with the lump that had me standing in front of the counter at my healthcare provider's network office, which is a part of a large and well-regarded medical center. For purposes of diplomacy I'm going to call it Our Lady of Perpetual Confusion Hospital System,* but it could have just as easily been Cedars of Confusion or Acme Med Center.

I was at the counter facing a clerk who was intently focused on the computer screen in front of her as she attempted to "find me" in the system. Her back was to a frosted-glass partition with the OLPCHS logo and a picture of a smiling, well-fed, comfortable middle-class couple frolicking healthily in an open field. I guess it was supposed to make me comfortable, to make me feel that such exuberant, bucolic activity was awaiting me as soon as I entered into the compassionate care of the OLPCHS system of hospitals and affiliated clinics. It was really good marketing.

Unfortunately, the glass also showed a reflection of her computer screen, which was lit up with an online shopping expedition for shoes. I told her my name, and she rearranged the screen to log me in. I provided my identification and my insurance card. I work for a pretty well-resourced group and have the good fortune of a "good" insurance plan, so what came next was a complete surprise.

"You have an outstanding balance," she said.

I wasn't sure if it was a statement, a challenge, or an icebreaker.

"For what?"

She then started to describe, in alarming detail, and with alarming volume, the diagnostics and purpose behind my last visit. Now had I not

*Our Lady of Perpetual Confusion Hospital System, or OLPCHS, is not to be confused with an existing healthcare system, private, secular, or faith-based, no matter how similar it seems to any existing network.

known any better, I would have just stood there mute and endured her disclosure—there were other people in line—of my medical condition. But I do know better.

"Uh, I think I am going to stop you, because that is my personal information. It's HIPAA** protected," I said. "I don't think it should be discussed in an open area like this."

Two other clerks' heads popped up from behind nearby computer monitors. I had used the magic acronym.

"I'm asking how much and what for, like one million dollars for lab work or something like that."

"It says a hundred and forty-nine dollars," she said.

My first thought was, what if I didn't have $149? What if I was in real pain? Or what if I was afraid about a diagnosis that might mean a foreshortened life and the wreckage of my dreams? What if I needed to work out how I would find and give them their $149 and wanted to discuss it and still leave the window with some shred of dignity left? The encounter was really offensive and degrading, and I actually have $149!

After asking a lot of questions, I learned that the "system" was posting a "cost" that had not yet been processed by my insurance provider. They also admitted, ultimately, that they did not expect me to pay it, but they had insinuated that I needed to before the current visit. The clerk knew all of this and could have offered it but was perfectly willing to let me pay out-of-pocket. It was a subtle coercion that had I not known to question would have victimized me.

About halfway through this discussion, I noticed the clerk in the next window was actively listening to the "private" conversation about both my financial issue and my medical history even though she neither was assisting me nor had any business other than personal curiosity.

When I asked "my" clerk if she was trying to say that I had to pay the pending balance before seeing the doctor about my lump, her coworker leaned toward the counter.

"I don't think you should ask her something like that," she said menacingly.

**HIPAA: Health Insurance Portability and Accountability Act of 1996, the patient privacy law.

Now I am not a shrinking violet. I don't like bullies, and I don't respond well to people trying to overwhelm logic with emotional ballistics. So I had a pretty good idea about what would happen when I very calmly said, "I don't think this is any of your business, ma'am."

I might as well have questioned the validity of her parents' marriage vows for the response it generated. In a flash she was out of her chair, leaving the other customers/patients in her line to wait. She crossed in front of the happy, healthy couple emblazoned on the frosted glass and, then realizing she would need some justification, caught herself and asked if I wanted to speak with a supervisor. It was obviously less about what I wanted and bore the hallmark of a threat.

I replied again calmly, because it was pretty clear that calm was going to be a rare commodity in the near future, "If it will help with your Q/A efforts, I am happy to be of service." Somehow she didn't seem appreciative.

By this point they had given up on trying to extract the $149 and were ready to take on the easier prey in line behind me. I was given my identity-hiding "number" by which I would be called to go to the examination room and took my place among the other newly processed, awaiting the good health experienced by the couple on the frosted glass. It dawned on me that with the hostility associated with having already accidentally disclosed my medical issues openly, the new numbering to protect my identity was very similar to the experience of being legally incarcerated. Name becomes number becomes identity!

I didn't have long to think about it, as the angry clerk returned to her enclosure. Just before leaving the waiting area, she pointed a finger at me and with a fairly threatening tone said, "The supervisor is going to talk to you!"

As we were beyond any interpersonal détente, I indulged myself by smiling and replying, "That sounds like a real hoot."

In retrospect, I found myself thinking that when it came to lumps, the one behind the counter was potentially far more malignant than the one behind my ear. Despite the outrageousness and impropriety of the people who were supposed to be helping me get to that state of cavorting healthily in a pasture, I was willing to let it all go.

I saw my care provider and came away with a treatment plan. He commiserated that a lot of people were relating an experience akin to a shake-down at the front desk, but that as he now worked for OLPCHS, there was little he could do about it.

I thanked him and let him off the hook for the emotional tag, but as I was walking out, I saw a woman, who had to be 80 years old, standing at that same counter. She was getting the same open-ended declaration of a balance due. She had on clothes that were of a dated style; although the material was not silk or linen, it was clean and pressed and she was "pulled together"—as my grandmother liked to say—for her visit to the doctor. She reminded me of a generation that I personally hold dear: accountable people who were honest and responsible and who believed that people in authority meant well and were trying to do right by them. She was embarrassed at the appearance that she had not paid her debt. Without questioning, she opened her worn, faux-leather purse and took out some folded bills.

All I could think was, "What if this makes a difference in what she is able to eat tonight?" Now I was mad. I stepped over to the elderly woman and said, "Ma'am, I couldn't help but overhear. Your insurance is probably still processing that amount, so you might just wait and see if you end up getting a bill. You don't have to pay anything right now, and it won't count against you."

She looked at me and then back at the clerk. The clerk gave me a look that said she'd like to give me a whole other reason to have to see the doctor, but the lady kept her money, and I felt as good as if I were cavorting with the couple in the field with $149 in my pocket.

Afterward I received a phone call from a nurse manager, who seemed more interested in why I was asking unsettling questions of the clerk than about a potential violation of privacy or dignity or insinuation of dead-beat status. We spoke for about 20 seconds before she concluded with her suggestion that "I could write a letter if I wanted to."

I asked if that would be helpful to her in addressing the issues that a patient (me) was bringing up. She said no, she had taken notes while we were talking. It didn't ring at all true. For one thing, it was all super quick and I talk fast. For another, she just didn't even sound like she cared. She really could have at least tried to sound more convincing. For $149 I expected a little better acting in our little theater of life. I resisted the impulse to ask if among her other professional accomplishments she was also a stenographer.

In any case, it was the wake-up call that something was terribly rotten in that state of health care, and instead of writing a letter, I might just put my pen to better use. This book is the result. I think now more than ever people need some form of advocacy or at least a guide to navigating some of the assaults they encounter when they are at their weakest, most vulnerable, and frightened.

These insights into the facts of the healthcare system and what you can do to better protect yourself will, I hope, make the journey a little less arduous. In doctor language, consider this book a prescription for self-empowerment. Throughout the book you will find tools that you can use to provide notification, capture medical information, and otherwise serve you as you deal with different aspects of the healthcare system. This is your book, and it is your health we are advocating. You should feel free to download the forms, tools, or guides from the accompanying website at http://www.PrepareToDefendYourselfHealth.com; photocopy them from this book; or even remove the page and use it that way. After all, this book is yours to use as you see fit.

As I started to research this book, I spoke with patients, government

Prescription for Self-empowerment

```
Your name:          Date of birth:        Address:


        Read the following book prn*

                (# 1)

   Refills: why not     Allergies: Hopefully not


      Generic substitution authorized: yes


                              Signed: Dr. X
```

    *(prn: Latin for pro re nata or literally: in the circumstance.
What it really means: As needed)

agencies, interest groups, lawmakers, and medical colleagues. I found that most people do not understand the intricacies and challenges of the current state of inpatient and outpatient care, hospitalization, health policy and law, emergency medical services, the business of medicine, and their own rights and obligations. This book is not by any means a comprehensive statement on any of those. It can be considered an introduction along with some fundamentals to help you take some control of your own journey through the healthcare system.

It's a primer: Healthcare Navigation 101.

I hope it helps.

I hope you make it out alive.

Matt Minson, MD

CHAPTER 1

THE LANGUAGE OF MEDICINE

SIT, STAY, DIAGNOSE!

Before I get too far into the specifics of self-empowerment in the system, I think it's helpful to begin with a brief history of medicine. Now, I can already see your eyelids starting to get heavy, but indulge me here. Knowing how the system got like this helps a lot in understanding *why* and *how* those who surround you and do unspeakable things to you in your moment of need view you, assess you, process you, talk to you, and ultimately what you can and can't do about it to protect yourself. Or to put it in the more elegant words of H. G. Wells, "History is a race between education and catastrophe."

As far as historians have been able to tell, by 4000 BC many religions had identified certain of their deities with healing. Without any understanding of the process of disease or how drugs worked, most believed that a person became ill because he or she had earned disfavor with the gods. Therefore, culpability, shame, and ostracism were quickly associated with illness. Sadly, this mentality sometimes holds over even today, especially in the areas of addiction and mental illness.

In particular, the temples of Saturn, and later of Asclepius in Asia Minor, became recognized as healing centers. People would travel to these "centers of healing" and offer prayers and sacrifices. Dream interpretations played a significant role in the ancient healing process (sounds kind of Jungian, doesn't it?), and much like the modern equivalent of social services support, the effects of the patient's daily life were considered to be paramount for a good outcome. Beyond the metaphysical, however, the priests or ancient physicians who attended and supported such practices also stitched wounds, set broken bones, and used narcotics—specifically opium—for pain.

On the surface it might seem that there weren't many similarities between the ancients and what we see today, but consider the following. In order to curry favor with the temperamental gods, supplicants (patients) would place offerings (co-pays) of animal flesh—say, a haunch of beef or a game bird—on a fiery altar of the respective god. This barbecued tribute also supported the lifestyle of the priests, who ate the cooked flesh. And that is the story of how we arrived at professional fees. As you can see, there were a lot of similarities to our current system even then.

These spiritually oriented hospitals were also structurally similar to what we now see in modern clinics, care centers, and hospitals. Plans for a fifth-century BC temple in Athens dedicated to Asclepius showed large rooms, 24 by 108 feet, for multiple dreamer-patients. This is amazingly close in dimension to its modern equivalent, the post-anesthesia care unit (PACU), or "recovery room."

On a similar note a network of Brahmanic hospitals were established in Sri Lanka as early as 431 BC, and King Ashoka of Hindustan established a chain of hospitals about 230 BC. These might well be the first examples of an organized healthcare system. Around 100 BC the Romans established specialized hospitals, the *valetudinaria*, to treat their sick and injured soldiers. This was just the early analog to our Veterans Administration hospitals. This was less a benevolent act than pure pragmatism. The soldiers' care was important because the vigor of the legions increased the perceived power of the empire.

Literary sources occasionally mention ancient hospitals, but only documents from Egypt reveal how widespread and even secular they were. *Testimonia* from the temples of Dendera, Thebes, and Memphis in Egypt record a multitude of hospitals founded by private individuals and independent of ecclesiastical or religious influence. These early records show that the origin of the hospital as an independent institution dedicated to medical care and not just as an offshoot of worship can be dated to the third quarter of the fourth century.

Most historians agree that the earliest example of the modern concept of a hospital dates from AD 331, when Emperor Constantine, having been converted to Christianity, abolished all pagan hospitals and created the opportunity for a new approach to caring for the ill. Until then, disease had spiritually isolated the sufferer from the community. This new Christian tradition emphasized the close relationship of the sufferer to his fellow humans, upon whom rested the obligation for care. Care of the sick thus became a benevolent matter for the church.

In the year AD 370 Saint Basil of Caesarea established a religious foundation in Cappadocia that looked remarkably like a modern medical center in its layout. It included a hospital, an isolation unit for those suffering from leprosy (an early sanitarium), and buildings to house the poor (early homeless shelters) and the elderly (retirement communities), as well as the sick ("laying-in" facilities and rehabilitation units). Following this example, an explosion of hospitals expanded into the eastern part of the

Roman Empire. Another notable accomplishment was that of Saint Benedict at Monte Cassino, founded early in the sixth century, where the care of the sick was placed above every other Christian duty, thus establishing a hierarchical obligation of care. It was from this beginning that one of the first medical schools in Europe was created at Salerno and was producing the finest medical practitioners in the world by the eleventh century. This example led to the establishment of similar monastic teaching infirmaries throughout the Western world.

Architecturally, the oldest evidence of a conventional hospital appears to be at Mihintale in Sri Lanka, which can be dated to the ninth century AD. The extensive ruins suggest there were patient rooms that measured 13 by 13 feet, which is surprisingly close to the dimensions of individual patient rooms today. The archeological dig of this site produced surgical instruments that would be recognizable to a modern surgeon. It also contained a stone "medicinal trough" approximately 7 feet long and 30 inches wide that may have been the first example of hydrotherapy using mineral water and medicinal oils.

In regard to the concepts of health care—co-pays, floor plans, and even our perceptions of illness—the more things change, the more they also seem to stay the same.

To fully understand the evolution of medical care, it is important to understand something about its politics and how it related to the crowned heads of the ancient world. I know what I am about to say next seems terribly absurd, but I think the best analogy can be found in taking a look at the *Brady Bunch.*

Prior to the Middle Ages, the system of primogeniture was set up to dictate the transfer of wealth and titles of nobility from generation to generation. This "law" stated that all wealth, property, and the endowment of power associated with title were to be passed on to a succession of children by order of birth, hence the term "heir apparent." The second son got nothing. Of course, if you think sibling rivalry is bad in the typical American family, then you can just imagine what it would be like if Jan Brady had just to kill off Marsha in order to become queen. Or if it works better, imagine Elizabeth I shrieking, "Marsha, Marsha, Marsha" right before she had Mary Queen of Scots beheaded.

Fortunately for the Bradys, the law of primogeniture generally applied mostly to males. In order to minimize the familial carnage and protect the throne, tradition dictated that the second son enter the military so the future king's top general had a strong family link. The third son went into the clergy so that all the powerful institutions of the developing world were covered for the royal family. With that in mind, Greg would be the heir apparent, Peter would go into the military, and Bobby would become a bishop or cardinal and therefore, the intellectual. I know what you are thinking, but you have to admit you won't ever forget the concept now.

Given what we have just learned about the progression of the temples of the healing gods to the religious custodianship of tending to the poor and the sick, the priestly evolution to *physick* or physician seemed only natural. The fact that the influential clergy/doctors were still tied to the royal family meant continued support and permanence for these new hospitals.

Fast-forward through the centuries: the church-based Hôtel-Dieu of Lyon was opened in AD 542, and the Hôtel-Dieu of Paris in AD 660. The monasteries had an *infirmitorium* (hence the term "infirmary"), a place where their sick were taken for treatment. They also cultivated gardens of medicinal plants and even had a primitive pharmacy where the plants were turned into cures. In addition to caring for sick monks and local parishioners, the monasteries opened their doors to pilgrims and other travelers. Think of this as akin to a spiritual traveler's health maintenance organization (HMO).

Religion continued to be the dominant influence in the establishment of European hospitals during the Middle Ages, as the growth of hospitals and systems of hospitals exponentially multiplied during the Crusades. Pestilence and disease were more potent enemies than the Saracens in defeating the crusaders, and massive military hospitals came into being along the traveled routes. The Knights Hospitalers of the Order of St. John in 1099 established a hospital in the Holy Land that could care for some 2,000 patients. It is said to have been especially concerned with eye diseases and may have been the first of the specialized hospitals. Even today this order exists as the St. John's Ambulance Corps.

In the Moorish territories of Spain and North Africa and throughout the Middle East, the Muslims established hospitals in Baghdad, Damascus, and Córdoba. These hospitals were notable because they admitted patients regardless of religious belief, race, or social order. This was a socially remarkable advancement in the accessibility of health care regardless of religious inclination, a philosophy that was not adopted until several hundred years later in Europe.

Around the same time the Hospital of the Holy Ghost, founded in 1145 at Montpellier in France, established a factually based and reproducible clinical curriculum and later became one of the most important centers in Europe for the training of physicians. This scientific school of thought was remarkably distinct from 2,000 monastic institutions under the Benedictines and the beginning of our model of medical training.

The Middle Ages also saw the beginnings of support for hospital-like institutions by secular authorities. Toward the end of the fifteenth century, many cities and towns recognized the value and supported some kind of institutional health care. It has been said that in England there were no fewer than 200 such establishments that met a growing social need. This gradual transfer of responsibility for institutional health care from the church to civil authorities continued in Europe, especially after the dissolution of the monasteries in 1540 by Henry VIII. Unfortunately, it also put an end to hospital building in England for some 200 years.

The loss of these monastic hospitals in England suddenly required that secular authorities provide for those who were sick, injured, or disabled, thus laying the foundation for the benevolence society or "voluntary hospital" movement. The first voluntary hospital in England was established around 1718 by Huguenots from France (go figure) and was closely followed by the foundation of such London hospitals as the Westminster in 1719, Guy's Hospital in 1724, and the London Hospital in 1740. Between 1736 and 1787, hospitals were established outside London in at least 18 cities. The initiative spread to Scotland, where the first voluntary hospital, the Little Hospital, was opened in Edinburgh in 1729. Given that it was in Scotland, I've always wondered why it wasn't called the "Wee Hospital," but I suppose it was to prevent people from confusing it with a urology center.

The first hospital in North America was built in Mexico City in 1524 by Hernán Cortés, and the structure still stands. The French established a hospital in Canada in 1639 at Quebec City, the Hôtel-Dieu du Précieux Sang, which is also still in operation, although not at its original location. In 1644 Jeanne Mance, a French noblewoman, built a hospital of ax-hewn logs on the island of Montreal, which was the beginning of the Hôtel-Dieu de St. Joseph, out of which grew the order of the Sisters of St. Joseph, now considered to be the oldest nursing group organized in North America. The first hospital in the territory of the present-day United States is said to have been a hospital for soldiers on Manhattan Island, established in 1663. These early American hospitals were offshoot alms-houses or charity centers, the first of which was established by William Penn in Philadelphia in 1713. The first incorporated hospital in America was the Pennsylvania Hospital, in Philadelphia, which obtained its charter from the Crown in 1751.

Now fast-forward to 1967—ignoring, of course, the development of X-rays, anesthesia, and penicillin—and medical history takes on a much more personal note. In Houston, Texas, a small boy sat in front of a television set watching the 1961 epic film *El Cid*, starring Charlton Heston and Sophia Loren. The small boy was me, and even at that age I had a real appreciation for Sophia Loren. There is a scene in the movie in which a group of people are cruel to a leper. I don't know if it really happened, but it is used in the film to illustrate the compassion of the Cid. For some reason the injustice of the leper's situation caused by his illness affected my six-year-old sensibility in a deep and disturbing way. I began crying sympathetically.

My mother came into the room from the kitchen with a look that said she would have believed me if I had claimed to have been stung by a scorpion or had eaten rat poison or been attacked by aliens. When she learned why I was carrying on so, the look on her face changed from alarm to one of matter-of-fact practicality, and, drying her hands on a dish towel, she offered a simple solution. "Maybe you can be a doctor someday, and you can help people like that."

She knew her son pretty well. I was a logic-driven creature even at the age of six, so with a plan I was able to cut off the waterworks and enjoy the rest of Sophia Loren. I owe a lot to that moment and to my mother . . . in many ways!

With my course in life decided, I immediately started paying more critical—and I am sure discomfiting—attention to my own doctor, Dr. Spencer. On my next visit I told him confidently that someday I was going to take over for him. I remember him patiently and a little exhaustedly looking around before saying, "Well, honey, you better hurry up."

Dr. Spencer was, like most back then, a family doctor. He knew us and cared for us from cradle to grave and was, in turn, crusty, brave, selfless, and compassionate—alternating perfectly between admonishing and nurturing. We valued him because he was uniquely capable and diagnostically accurate and astute. He addressed the basic problems with us and was not distracted by the short goal of just alleviating our symptoms. When we were not at our best, he thought for us and was an objective mentality who saw us through to cure. He patiently bore our complaints, our uninformed self-determination and diagnosis, and at times our misguided attitudes. With his usual focus, objectivity, and calm, he even put up with the fact that we often had, by ill-advised behaviors, caused our own problems. He was uniquely heroic.

In those days medical technology was relatively primitive, and the clinician's inherent diagnostic abilities were, by necessity, arguably better than they are today. Doctors relied on the "history" taken from a patient. This included the chief complaint or why one was seeking care, the history of the present illness, any past medical history, and associated social elements, like smoking and drinking. It also included a secondary checklist called a review of systems and then, ultimately, a physical examination to narrow the "differentials" or possible diagnoses.

Already you can see that this takes some time and attention and is better served by a methodical thought process, not the hurried and time-pressured questionnaire we often experience today.

Unlike today, Dr. Spencer and his peers were predominantly generalists. Think family doctors and primary-care "specialists." They were the gatekeepers, the quarterbacks of our care, keeping an overarching eye on all of our medications and surgeries so that no negative interactions could occur. Medical specialists and subspecialists were in the minority. By the time I was starting medical school, an explosion in technological tools such as computerized tomography (CT scans), magnetic resonance imaging (MRI), and more had given doctors the ability to "look" rather than "ask." A natural but unfortunate development was a trend toward less attention to interaction with the patient and more "processing" of the data. On top of that, the new "business" element of health care put increased value on physician speed and expedited turnover. As a result the valuable time and interaction between caregiver and patient was even further reduced.

With the emphasis on technology, and the financial incentives of sub-specialization, physicians began proportionally moving away from primary care. It's not difficult to understand. According to the Bureau of Labor Statistics, primary-care physicians earn an average of $202,392 a year, while physicians in specialties earn an average of $356,885 a year. According to a Merritt Hawkins survey, family practitioners earn an average $173,000 annually, while neurosurgeons earn an average $571,000. That's minuscule compared to what these physicians generate for hospitals, so there is even more encouragement for them to subspecialize.

As you can imagine, when a caregiver's scope of practice becomes more focused on a specific disease process, it is not as focused on the individual experiencing it. With more specialization came even more compartmentalization, and the patient care process became disengaged and impersonal, with patients often left wondering who was really taking care of them.

A similar explosion in pharmacological advancements made the patient's care much more complex and made it even more necessary for someone to have overall clinical awareness and control. The truth is that now, with all of the healthcare system's sophistication, the best custodian of your care is you.

In order to make sure that you can be a good custodian of your care, it helps to understand how your physician or caregiver thinks and how he processes the information you discuss. With apologies to my colleagues, think about talking with us, caregivers, like you do when you are house-training a puppy. If you don't know how a puppy thinks and processes a command or information, you won't get your message across, and that means bad news for your carpet.

So what can you do? You can communicate your issues and problems effectively so that your caregiver understands. After all, the practice of medicine is really about communicating, at least it is for the purpose of arriving at a diagnosis. So with that in mind, let's talk about something called the "SOAP note."

From the very moment a normal human being enters medical school, he or she is indoctrinated to a way of communicating and thinking that is almost completely alien to that of the rest of the world. The origins for such training and communication go all the way back to a rigorous and ancient form of instruction and an equally distant language, Latin. Knowing what you now do about the evolution of American medicine and its derivation from liturgical origins, it sort of makes sense. That said, I have always found it ironic and potentially disturbing that the terminology used to maintain my health and preserve my life comes from a "dead" language.

When a physician begins to interview a patient (you), he does so with a sequence of information gathering that is commonly known as a SOAP note, or "Subjective, Objective, Assessment, and Plan." It is also how the information is recorded so that it makes sense to another medical provider. Interestingly, this format is almost universally used regardless of country.

Subjective

The Subjective section is the part of the chart that captures the information given by you, the patient. It's an interview, basically. It is composed of the chief complaint, the history of present illness, and any past medical history. By having this sequence of information organized in your own mind as a patient, you will be better assured that the caregiver has what he needs to know in order to figure out what is wrong with you. From there the caregiver can take the appropriate action and treat you more accurately and quickly, and who doesn't want that? So here is how the physician will approach you.

CHIEF COMPLAINT

This is what a caregiver calls the primary thing that a patient states when needing care. It is often loaded into the patient record, *your record*, in quotation marks. Why is this important? As the old adage says, you only get one chance at a first impression. In order to make sure that you help your caregiver, think about what is the problem. If it is one thing, great. If more than one, say so, but try to be organized and clear. I'll give you an example of what I mean.

I once had a patient named Mrs. Gilhooley. That is not her real name. You should understand up front that I liked Mrs. Gilhooley a lot. She was a smart and informed patient, but anytime I picked up a chart and I saw her name, I invariably braced myself for a frustrating and futile experience. When it came to getting a cogent history, Mrs. Gilhooley was a challenge.

She was what my favorite psychiatry colleague calls a "tangential talker." The way I would describe it is that Mrs. Gilhooley answered questions the way Christopher Columbus navigated the globe. She goes way, way, wayyyyy west to arrive in the East. As Columbus learned, by doing that, you don't always get where you want to be and it's certainly not fast.

I pulled back the curtain around the stretcher and found Mrs. Gilhooley seated, looking fairly distressed. Her hairpiece was barely hanging on to her head at a strange angle and looked a little like it had recently come to life and was trying to make its escape. As far as I was concerned, if it came down to a struggle between Mrs. Gilhooley and a semi-animated hairpiece, my money was on Mrs. Gilhooley.

I shook off the desire to contemplate that anymore and looked down at what I assumed was the real reason for her visit. Her foot was propped up on a pillow, and her great toe was the size and color of a ripe plum. I could tell she had taken a fall, and I was already thinking about what I needed to do for her when I asked the fateful question.

"What brings you in today, Mrs. Gilhooley?"

"Well," she said, "I was over at the Food King this morning . . . My son and his family are in town for the weekend, you see . . . He's a lawyer, but not malpractice law . . . Anyway his wife won't eat anything with gluten . . . It's not that she is intolerant; she just doesn't like it . . ."

"She didn't do this to you?" I asked, hoping to put something of a rudder in the ocean of her story.

She looked at me like I was some startlingly ludicrous simpleton. "Heavens, no! She's a lovely person, though she does have a temper sometimes . . . I told my son that when they got married, but you know you can't tell him anything . . . Anywayyyyy, he loves pancakes and I was at the store getting gluten-free pancake mix . . . which is no small feat, let me tell you . . ."

I had lost all hope of control and decided to go along on the journey with her.

"Well," she said, "I got home after hunting all over for gluten-free pancake mix, and there she was, in the kitchen, already making pancakes . . . with regular old flour . . . I was so distracted by that that I accidentally kicked the doorway with my big toe and took a tumble . . . It really hurts."

"You fell," I said. "Did you hit your head?"

She reached up, felt the hairpiece, and realized it was misaligned. "Oh no, not at all, I just realized my 'fall' is crooked."

"Your wig, there, you mean?" I asked.

"Wig? Heaven's no, I'm not bald; it's just a fall, just a little beauty enhancement . . ."

Here's how it ended up on the chart: "Sixty-nine-year-old female presents with a chief complaint of, 'I accidentally kicked the doorway.' Patient admits to fall, but denies other pain or injury."

The reason I am telling you this is to illustrate that when it came to getting good care, Mrs. Gilhooley really didn't help herself. I am comfortable that she got it eventually, but it was a lot like taking a cruise with Captain Columbus.

So what is my point? That patients don't know how to talk to their medical provider? Well, actually, with respect, yes.

WHAT YOU CAN DO

As I mentioned before, if you were going to house-train a puppy, you would consider that canines have a certain way of thinking, and by knowing what works in the thought process of the dog, you could communicate your wishes properly and reduce your upholstering bill at the same time. We medical providers are just like that, only, for the most part, bipedal.

We have certain keywords and triggers that for a puppy might be *sit*, *stay*, or *no* but are equally meaningful to us when you say *onset*, *severity*, and *duration*. So the following section will help in organizing your thoughts to their/our way of thinking, and don't be afraid to take notes. Review as you take notes and study the text box at the end of this chapter, "What Your Doctor Needs to Know." Cut it out and laminate it if you want. You won't hurt my feelings.

Regardless of how you approach communicating, what you say will influence the direction the care provider goes in further questioning or in this
section of the medical questionnaire or chart, History of Present Illness.
This is a very important part of the discussion between you and your
doctor and is where you can make a significant difference in how well he
understands your problem and what to do to help you. Here are some
things that will help your caregiver help you:

- *When* did the problem start? To physicians the onset of an illness
  is as critically important a piece of information as the way it
  started. Think back to when you first noticed the problem, not
  just when it became severe enough to seek help. For Mrs. Gilhooley, she might begin, "About two hours ago . . ."
- Was it *a sudden onset* or *gradual*? Has it stayed the same or worsened or come and gone? How long is the interval between
  waves, episodes, or spells? If it is a recurring or a chronic problem, be clear about when the most recent episode began. If it is
  an injury, describe the circumstance. Mrs. Gilhooley might then
  continue, "About two hours ago, I struck my big toe on the
  doorjamb."
- *Where* is it, and where did it start? If they are same, be sure to say
  that. If the sensation, pain, or area affected has changed (grown,
  or swelled, or shrunk), try to describe that as completely as
  possible. If the sensation is a painful one, try to describe the
  quality of it. Is it *sharp, dull, electric, aching, throbbing, deep,* or
  at the *surface,* or a combination? Mrs. Gilhooley might respond,
  "About two hours ago, I struck my big toe on the doorjamb,
  and my toe is really throbbing."
- Does the sensation or pain *radiate* or extend *beyond the immediate area affected?* Think about how the chest pain caused by
  a heart attack often has associated pain "traveling" down the
  arm. Mrs. Gilhooley would then go on, "About two hours ago, I
  struck my big toe on the doorjamb, and my toe is really throbbing, but that's the only thing that hurts."

- Is there a *pattern*? If it is pain, does it hurt before movement, with movement, or after? If it's, say, nausea, do you get nauseated after you eat? Before you eat? Every morning? Mrs. Gilhooley might finally say, "About two hours ago, I struck my big toe on the doorjamb, and my toe is really throbbing, but that's the only thing that hurts. Of course, I can't stand on it or move it, because of the pain."
- Are there *associated symptoms*, meaning other complaints? As Shakespeare wrote, "When sorrows come, they come not single spies, but in battalions." The same is applicable to illness. Rare and fortunate are the cases in which only one issue plagues a patient. Even something straightforward like a twisted ankle has to be investigated for associated problems such as numbness (indicating possible nerve injury) or pale toes (blood-flow issues).

PAST MEDICAL HISTORY

Once finished with the history of recent illness, the caregiver will ask about your past medical history, any surgeries, allergies, and what medications you are taking. He may ask about social issues such as alcohol consumption, smoking, or other personal issues. Finally, he will run down a quick anatomical systems checklist, called a review of systems, to catch anything else. And that is it.

So, when you approach a healthcare provider, remember that he or she is ever more technologically dependent and time-pressured by the business requirements of medicine. You can better serve yourself and help the caregiver help you by having your thoughts organized in the fashion that best communicates to him. This successful communication hopefully will not be critical, but it certainly could be. Be good to yourself. Help your caregiver.

Objective

The Objective section of the chart is all the stuff your doctor determines by examination. This includes your vital signs: your pulse, blood pressure, temperature, and respiration count (how many times you breathe in a minute), and your *physical examination*. This examination may be a comprehensive examination of *you*. That is what you should expect from your primary-care provider. If you are in an emergency department, depending on your history of present illness, the examination may be confined to just the injured area, what providers call a *focused examination*. This explains in part why sprained ankles don't generally lead to a pelvic exam. Focused examinations are not bad things, but they do carry the risk of missing something. So, once again, be aware, and if there is something you think should be looked at ("observed"), touched ("palpated"), or listened to ("auscultated), speak up. This is, after all, about you taking control and being a member—maybe the most invested member—of your care team.

The Objective section on the chart will also include the results of any laboratory tests (blood, urine, or other specimens taken from you) and/or radiological tests (X-rays, CT scans, MRIs, etc.).

I'm going to take a quick moment to distinguish between two words that are often used—even by providers—incorrectly. *Symptoms* are what you feel. *Signs* are objective findings discovered by the healthcare provider during your examination. For example, abdominal pain is something you feel and thus is a symptom. Abdominal tenderness is elicited when your abdomen is "palpated," or mashed by the examiner. Tenderness is a sign.

And one more thing: Make sure the healthcare provider uses a manual cuff, not the machine, the first time your blood pressure is taken.

Assessment

The Assessment portion is the written conclusion of the caregiver and may include not just the cause of your problem, or *diagnosis*, but other conclusions that may affect your health. If the exact cause of your problem is not immediately evident, the caregiver will record something called a *differential diagnosis*. This is just a list of the possible medical causes or problems in the descending order of likelihood. I am including this because I strongly advocate that patients retain a copy of their medical records in case of travel, the need for a new provider, and in the interest of their own survival.

Knowing how to read your chart is critical in maintaining empowerment in the ever-compartmentalized system. Decoding the assessment is important so that you can speak with clarity and assurance. If you don't understand something, ask your caregiver to explain it. If he won't or can't, maybe you should rethink your relationship. Think of it like this: If you took your car to a repair shop, and the mechanic walked out and said there was something wrong—you have a broken "spetzer valve" (this happened to me and I'm not even sure there is such a thing), and I need $1,000 to fix it—wouldn't you ask for more information, such as what exactly *is* a spetzer valve? Your life and health are just as important, right? Often though, we just trust the speaker, or worse, are too intimidated to question. You shouldn't be. It's your body, and you have every right to demand that your caregiver makes sure you understand.

Plan

The Plan is why you came to these people in the first place to get whatever is bothering you fixed or clarified. Often patients don't feel they have a right to question the plan or even inquire further. After all, you are sick and want to get on with it. Then again, you have every right to know what is coming . . . in detail. Again, don't hesitate to ask. Include items like these: What are the risks of my condition? What is the recovery rate? Will I be 100 percent or partial from now on? Is this a one-time thing? Is there anything else I/you can do? By doing this, you will be, if not the master, then at least an informed participant in your own medical fate. And that is really what you should be after.

A lot of this chapter has been about communication and what you can do to enhance it. There is one last bit of communication you are likely to have well after you have left a clinic or emergency department. How you respond to it will probably not only have an effect on your care but will also affect the care of others and may even affect medical practice in the future.

If you have been sick in the last few years, you have most likely noticed the number of consumer surveys you've received. They probably far outnumber the communications regarding laboratory test results or clinical follow-up you've received. Unfortunately, most of these surveys seem more focused on your perception and mood rather than the objectives.

What Your Doctor Needs to Know from You

THE SOAP NOTE

SUBJECTIVE
- Chief complaint (main problem)
- History of the present illness or injury
    Where is it? Has it moved or changed?
    When did it start? Gradual or sudden?
    Quality? Sharp, dull, aching, shocking, deep, shallow?
- Past medical history (allergies, medications, surgeries)

OBJECTIVE
- Vital signs (pulse, blood pressure, breathing rate per minute)
- Physical examination
- Laboratory and radiology tests

ASSESSMENT
- Differential diagnosis

PLAN
- What is the doctor going to do about it?

They emphasize pleasantries and perception, which are important, but not at the expense or exclusion of diagnosis, clinical excellence, and cure.

In my review of a sample of emergency department consumer surveys, quick administration of pain medication is a priority, as is "Did you feel welcome?" However, "Were you properly diagnosed" was not a component of any of those sampled. Neither was "Were they able to get your IV started in three attempts or fewer," or "Were you cured?"

I often think about the curmudgeonly care from Dr. Spencer that saw me through my childhood illnesses and wonder how he would fare today with the new emphasis on patient satisfaction or, for lack of a better term, happiness. Remembering him as I do, I imagine Dr. Spencer would remind me that even the overly bold, risk-taking Founders only dared promise the *pursuit* of happiness, and to expect a hospital to achieve it is a bit of an overreach.

If a doctor nowadays were to take on the same demeanor as Dr. Spencer, that person would likely be misunderstood, undervalued, and driven out by the bureaucracy. You see, he could chide me to get more exercise, stop smoking (if I smoked), get off the couch and exercise more, and eat less. It would be more personal, valued, and effective than any 10-second spot on television preaching similarly. It is as different as your mother telling you not to play with matches and a public service announcement. Both are useful, but I'm fairly certain that despite her tone, Mom cares more about me than a network.

Thanks, Mom.

Oh, and if you find out what the spetzer valve is, please let me know.

CHAPTER 2

MEDICAL PROFESSIONALS

YOU CAN'T TELL THE PLAYERS
WITHOUT A PROGRAM

YEARS LATER, WILLARD WOULD PROVE THE ASSERTION THAT GREAT OBSTETRICIANS ARE BORN NOT MADE

It has been famously said that "there is no place you can't go with a clipboard and a confident wave." If someone is wearing a uniform or carrying the accoutrements of authority, we tend to accept that the person is *in* authority. Put that in the hospital setting, and factor in that you are in pain or ill and far from at your best. Someone in scrubs and a lab coat becomes what you need her to be, your healthcare expert and proxy. The question is, who is this person and how qualified is she to do that?

What are her credentials and qualifications? What does getting to that level of credential really mean? What is her experience? In the course of treatment you will potentially interact with medics, nurses, practitioners, assistants, and specialists of varying stripes. It can be really confusing as to who is authorized and properly trained to determine and perform different tasks, and that is even before you get a sedative! The fact is that we trust this person in uniform, often without knowing her backstory.

The compartmentalization of medicine has been mentioned previously, so it helps for you to have an idea of who you are talking to and what that person's role is in the healthcare system.

Physicians

I intentionally use the term "physician" here, because it distinguishes a medical doctor (a graduate of a medical school) from other "doctors" (doctors of philosophy). The term "doctor" can be quite broad, and a doctor in the healthcare setting may be a doctor of education, nursing, physics, or English literature. Imagine your English teacher holding a scalpel, and you see the importance of this concept.

A *licensed physician* is a graduate of a medical school or osteopathic medical school who has met certain postgraduate requirements for licensure and the privilege to practice medicine. What makes a medical education distinct from a nursing education, or technical medical training, is the method, content, and structure of the training.

Technically, a graduate of a medical or osteopathic medical school is a physician, but until that individual has completed an internship and passed certain examinations, he cannot obtain a license. Until those postgraduate requirements are met, an individual is a *medical* or *osteopathic doctor*, but not a licensed physician.

For most American-educated physicians, the training progression is as follows. They graduate from high school or obtain a GED, and then they graduate from college with a requirement to take certain classes in mathematics, physics, chemistry, organic chemistry, and biology, with a grade-point average that generally must be above a minimum of 3.5 out of 4.0. They then undergo a competitive process (including a competitive entry examination known as the Medical College Admissions Test or MCAT) in order to get into medical school. They must then graduate from medical school, during which time they must take certain qualifying examinations (boards) to progress to clinical (patient care) training and then compete for entrance to an internship or residency. Internship and residency placement are also competitive processes, with grade-point averages, exam scores, and subjective evaluations weighing heavily. Internship and residency are intense training periods that involve patient care—as a

practicing physician—and continuing book study within a supervised setting. The oversight is provided by autonomous, licensed, board-certified physicians known as *attendings*. Internship lasts one year. Residency is specialized training (family medicine, emergency medicine, dermatology, surgery, etc.) that may last, depending on the specialty, three to five years. Beyond that some physicians will engage in additional formal training known as a fellowship that generally lasts a year. In order to advance year to year, certain success measures (testing and evaluations) must be met.

Internal medicine physicians, or "internists," are not to be confused with "interns." Interns are first-year postgraduates, but internists are specialists, although a doctor can be an intern in internal medicine; so you *do* need a program to know the players, and that is just the physicians.

Some residencies are listed as "competitive," meaning they eliminate or whittle down the number of residents each year. This is pretty stressful in that a resident may be eliminated even though the individual has done a good job. He or she must then reapply to another program or specialty and start all over again. The one positive characteristic of this part of the training process for the physician is that the resident is actually getting paid a salary or stipend by the training program or medical school.

This is usually a remarkably small amount. In 2011 the average ranged from $40,000 to $50,000. That may sound like a lot, but the resident is generally working from 60 to 80 hours a week. This amounts to a pay rate of $10 to $16 dollars an hour. Consider that during "off" time the resident is still required to continue study, and it amounts to a pretty austere financial situation.

During this period of time the student loans that have accrued may be deferred until the completion of training, though interest is still building. During college and medical school, students have been paying for their education and often have accrued substantial debt with no guarantee that they will graduate or end up in their chosen specialty.

To put this in context, the average college graduate enters the work environment with student loans from college and begins earning, hopefully. If the person is responsible, he or she will begin paying the loan down and start saving for retirement. A physician has another four years of debt accruement and then at least four to six years of subsistence earning, before entering any financial productivity. Generally, physicians will eventually earn more, but there are additional factors that affect those earnings, including the malpractice insurance costs for potential civil and liability risks. Why am I telling you this? As in most things, the backstory puts things in perspective.

After residency, most physicians will begin practice as *board-eligible* specialists. In a specialty, physicians must have completed their residency to call themselves a specialist and begin a practice. A *board-certified* physician has completed the specialty (residency) training and then (when that is passed successfully) must pass a written examination and (when that is passed successfully) must pass a verbal examination. Some physicians also engage in further study, or *fellowships,* in which subspecialization is emphasized.

After going through all this, a licensed physician is considered *autonomous as a practitioner* or able to function and exercise *judgment* in the practice of medicine without oversight. The licensed physician is still accountable to conduct and regulatory requirements and is subject to actions by state medical boards, regulatory agencies, and the law of the land. Only a state medical board can revoke a license. In order to maintain a license, a physician must meet certain continuing medical education requirements and behavior.

Malpractice insurance is generally carried by all advanced health practitioners, not just physicians. This is strictly for civil rather than legal protection. Certain specialties, because of the potential impact of the types of issues they address (orthopedics, neurosurgery, anesthesiology, trauma surgery, obstetrics) and the potential for large civil losses, have higher premiums. There have been numerous discussions about tort reform, which would limit the maximum amount of an award against doctors, nurses, paramedics, emergency medical technicians (EMTs), ambulance services, hospitals, healthcare corporations, and the like. Other books rightly, and much more comprehensively, focus on this subject. It is included here only to illustrate the number of influences that affect a clinical practice.

Specialists

A specialist is a physician who has completed an internship and residency in a focused area of care. Specialties are basically divided into the categories "internal medicine" and "surgical."

I have a colleague (a famous internal medicine specialist) who likes to say that "internists know everything and do nothing and surgeons don't know anything and do everything." An orthopedist (bone doctor) I used to work with liked to describe the ideal orthopedic resident candidate as "strong as a mule and *twice* as smart!" It's a lie, as most of them were tops in the medical school class, but it's pretty funny.

The only thing I can add to this is my favorite joke about medical specialists. One day an internist, a surgeon, and a family practitioner decide to go duck hunting together. As they sit in the blind, a flock of birds flies overhead. The internist looks up and says, "Rule out duck, rule out goose, rule out pigeon," then grabs a copy of the Audubon bird guide and starts to read as the flock flies away. A little while later, another flock appears. The surgeon leaps up and fires before yelling, "Rule out duck!" After some time, another group of birds flies over. The family practitioner says nothing but jumps up, blasting away. As several birds fall into the water, he says, "I have no idea what they were, but I got them." Absurdly exaggerated? Probably.

Specialties may also be classified as diagnostic (obtaining the diagnosis) or therapeutic. Specialties are also created to address specific diseases or organ systems of the body or to address different ages. For example, physicians that treat diseases of the endocrine system are endocrinologists. Organ system–based specialties are for diseases of a specific organ. Treatment of diseases of the skin is rendered by dermatologists. Age-related specialties might focus on childhood disease (neonatologists, pediatricians, etc.). Combined specialties are also encountered, such as age-specific specialties and surgical correction of an age group's maladies (pediatric surgery). Specialties can also be based on just a surgical technique, for example, a hand surgeon. While it is not comprehensive, table 1 gives some common examples.

Hospitalists

This is a new specialty of medicine, but one that is likely to have the greatest impact on the future of your care in the years to come. This is also unprecedented as a specialty in that it does not follow any of the previously mentioned principles with regard to specialization. It is also a

Table 1. Specialties and subspecialties

Specialty	Can be sub-specialty of this specialty	Diagnostic (D) or thera-peutic (T) specialty	Surgical (S) or internal medicine specialty (I)	Age range of patients	Organ based (O) or tech-nique based (T)
Allergy and immunology	Pediatrics or internal medicine	Both	I	All	O
Anesthetics	None	T	S	All	T
Cardiology	Internal medicine	T	I	Adults	O
Cardiothoracic surgery	General surgery	T	S	Adults	O
Child and adolescent psychiatry and psychotherapy	None	T	I	Pediatric	O
Clinical neurophysiology	Neurology	D	I	All	Both
Dermato-venereology	None	T	I	All	O
Endocrinology	Internal medicine	T	I	Adults	O
Gastroenterology	Internal medicine	T	I	Adults	O
General surgery	None	T	S	Variable	T
Geriatrics	Internal medicine	T	I	Geriatric	Multidisciplinary
Gynecology and obstetrics	None	T	S	All	O
Health informatics	None	T, D	Neither	All	Multidisciplinary
Infectious diseases	Internal medicine	T	I	Variable	Neither
Internal medicine	None	T	I	Adults	Neither
Interventional radiology	Radiology	T	Both	All	Multidisciplinary
Microbiology	None	D	I	All	T
Neonatology	Pediatrics	T	I	Neonatal	Neither
Nephrology	Internal medicine	T	I	Adults	O
Neurology	None	T	I	Adults	O
Neuroradiology	Radiology	D	I	All	Both
Neurosurgery	None	T	S	All	O
Nuclear medicine	None	D	I	All	T
Occupational medicine	None	T	I	Working age	Multidisciplinary
Ophthalmology	None	T	S	All	O
Oro-maxillo-facial surgery	Several	T	S	All	O

Table 1, continued

Orthopedics	General surgery	T	S	All	O
Otorhinolaryngology	None	T	S	All	O
Pathology	None	D	Neither	All	T
Pediatric allergology	Pediatrics	T	I	Pediatric	O
Pediatric cardiology	Pediatrics	T	I	Pediatric	O
Pediatric endocrinology and diabetes	Pediatrics	T	I	Pediatric	O
Pediatric gastroenterology, hepatology, and nutrition	Pediatrics	T	I	Pediatric	O
Pediatric hematology and oncology	Pediatrics	T	I	Pediatric	O
Pediatric infectious diseases	Pediatrics	T	I	Pediatric	O
Pediatric nephrology	Pediatrics	T	I	Pediatric	O
Pediatric respiratory medicine	Pediatrics	T	I	Pediatric	O
Pediatric rheumatology	Pediatrics	T	I	Pediatric	O
Pediatric surgery	General surgery	T	S	Pediatric	O
Pediatrics	None	T	I	Pediatric	Neither
Physical and rehabilitation medicine	None	T	I	Adults	Multidisci-plinary
Plastic, reconstructive, and aesthetic surgery	General surgery	T	S	All	O
Pneumology	Internal medicine	T	I	Adults	O
Psychiatry	Internal medicine	T	I	Adults	T
Public health	None	Neither	Neither	All	T
Radiology	None	D	I	All	T
Radiotherapy	Radiology	T	Neither	All	T
Urology	General surgery	T	S	All	O
Vascular medicine	Internal medicine	T	I	Adults	O
Vascular surgery	General surgery	T	S	All	O

specialty created by hospitals and the healthcare system and the first that reflects an institutional job description rather than a disease process, organ system, age group, or technique. This is important, as it notes a significant departure in the role of a physician in the system. Unlike your primary-care physician in a traditional practice whom you choose, who bills you or your insurance, and then follows you in a hospital if you have to be admitted, the hospitalist is on shift at the hospital and is assigned to cover all admissions during a certain period. (Hospitalists are different from "intensivists," who specialize in the management of critically ill patients in intensive care units [ICUs].) In the traditional primary-care physician-patient relationship, the patient (you) is the consumer and the physician is accountable to you. The hospitalist is accountable to the hospital for whom he or she works. When the hospitalist goes off-shift, another hospitalist coming on-shift takes that person's place. Hospitalists are also compensated differently. They draw a salary and sometimes a bonus from the hospital. This is not directly based on services provided to you and paid by your insurance carrier, Medicare, or Medicaid. In general, hospitalists are internal medicine physicians by training, although other specialties are represented. A small number have also completed a fellowship.

Hospitals and healthcare systems endorse the hospitalist as an improvement in cost effectiveness. The drawbacks are that the hospitalist will not have the same familiarity with an admitted patient, and in order to assure the best care, the hospitalist will need to have an effective and seamless line of communication with your primary-care provider. A number of studies have been done with regard to use of hospitalists. They have, admittedly, been focused primarily on cost and shortened hospital stay and are not as definite in their conclusions regarding quality of care, readmission, and some other clinical elements. As this is a new specialty, it will be interesting to see what future studies find regarding the impact on the quality of care.

Physician Assistants

Physician assistants (PAs) are probably some of the most misunderstood players in the advanced practitioner environment. Their privileges of practice and authority (narcotic prescription and physician oversight of medical care) vary considerably from state to state, and there is currently a great deal of activity in state legislatures that will affect how broadly and how autonomously PAs can practice. I have trained and practiced alongside PAs and believe they are extremely valuable members of the "physician extender" group of practitioners, which includes advanced practice nurses or nurse practitioners. The biggest difference is that PAs are philosophically trained similarly to physicians in a manner known as the "medical model."

In general a PA's progression of training is as follows. The individual graduates from high school or obtains a GED, then graduates from college with a requirement to take certain classes in mathematics, physics, chemistry, organic chemistry, biology, biochemistry, human anatomy, genetics—courses similar to the types a premed student must take. There are science classes geared toward those entering a medical profession (PA or MD), and they are substantially more demanding than what anyone else has to take. As a rule, PAs must have attained a grade-point average of 3.0 on a 4.0 scale. They then undergo a competitive process (including a competitive entry examination known as the Graduate Records Examination or GRE) in order to get into a physician's assistant school. In addition, most programs require that the applicant have 2,000 hours of clinical experience before entering PA training.

Physician assistant education includes classroom and laboratory instruction in subjects such as pathology, human anatomy, physiology, clinical medicine, physical diagnosis, and medical ethics. The programs also include supervised clinical training in several areas, including family medicine, internal medicine, emergency medicine, and pediatrics. Many programs have clinical teaching affiliations with medical schools. The training involves a mixture of classroom and clinical modules during the first two years, with clerkships during the third, culminating in a bachelor's and master's degree in physician assistant studies. More specifically, 9–15 months of the program are spent in supervised clinical training, according to the Physician Assistant Education Association (PAEA) and the American Academy of Physician Assistants (AAPA).

Following this training, the PA can begin practicing medicine, which involves seeing patients, determining diagnoses, and carrying out treatment plans under a physician's supervision. This is known as practicing under a *supervisory agreement* with the physician. In most states PAs have

The Medical Model

The medical model is focused on the determination of a differential diagnosis and definitive diagnosis, based on the history and physical exam. It uses this method to determine what additional laboratory and radiological tests are necessary toward achieving this goal.

This has some bearing on the philosophy of the players in modern health care because even today their origins and the traditional nature of their jobs affect how they are trained. Physicians and physician assistants are trained according to the medical model. Nurse training has been traditionally geared more toward the execution of a care plan, which is determined by the physician. It includes less diagnostic responsibility and places more emphasis on the comfort of and psychological attention to a patient, which is vital. As advanced practice for nurse professionals has received greater emphasis, more elements of the medical model's philosophy are included but also require some adjustment. Ideally for the patient, the roles of physicians and nurses are complementary when performed correctly.

100 percent of their patient charts reviewed by the physician within 24 hours, although the requirements actually vary depending on the rules established by each state's legislature.

Physician assistants may work in a wide variety of clinical specialties, everything from primary care to pediatrics and general surgical care. The PAEA annual report describes the following distribution of PAs by specialty: Family/General Medicine (36 percent); General Surgery & Surgical Subspecialties (20 percent); Internal Medicine & IM Subspecialties (17 percent); Emergency Medicine (10 percent); Pediatrics (4 percent); Ob/Gyn (3 percent); and Other (10 percent). The report also describes the distribution of PAs by work setting as follows: Hospital (37 percent);

Group Practice (27 percent); Ambulatory Care (11 percent); Solo MD Practice (10 percent); Other Settings (10 percent); and HMO/Managed Care (4 percent).

Nurse Practitioners

Nurse practitioners or advanced practice nurses, depending on the state, are another example of a physician extender. For most nurse practitioners, the training progression is as follows. They graduate from high school or obtain a GED and then graduate from a program in which they earn a bachelor of science in nursing (BSN) degree. Then they apply to and enter an advanced nurse practitioner program and graduate with a master of science degree in nursing (MSN). The training in the nurse practitioner program is generally very focused training in one area of care and does not follow the medical model specifically. Those areas usually include nurse midwifery (obstetrical care), primary-care nurse practitioners, clinical nurse specialists, and nurse anesthetists. At least one year of clinical experience is required prior to entering the advanced practitioner program, but in most cases nurses have much more work experience as a BSN registered nurse before they enter the advanced training track.

As you can imagine, this particular physician extender advanced practice is some of the most difficult to generalize, and for you as a patient it is also the most important to determine in order to assure your own best care. In some states and in some practice arrangements the nurse practitioner must have physician oversight, but the type of oversight varies. The biggest adjustment in advanced practice for nurses is that from regular nursing care, which does not traditionally determine the patient's diagnosis or the remedy. Ironically, the requirements of physician supervision that reside with physician assistants do not always exist for nurse practitioners, even though their scope is often specialty finite and does not originate from the medical model style of training. This statement is not meant to place either physician extender in a superior position but to show their different paths in arriving at advanced practice.

In order to be fully informed, consult your state's medical and nursing boards to determine what rules of oversight apply and whether your nurse practitioner is acting on a protocol with a supervisory physician relationship or more independently. The description of the "independent" nurse practitioner is fairly misunderstood. Nurse practitioners are "independent" in that their nursing license is issued by the respective state nursing board; however, the "collaborative practice" arrangement that permits these MSNs to perform is a de facto supervisory arrangement with a physician or physician practice. This is true in most states. Only in rare circumstances would one find a nurse practitioner practicing medicine without some definite connection to a physician's oversight.

The specific titles, credentials, and postnominal initials that nurse practitioners utilize will vary greatly by state, license type, academic degree, and nursing certification. Postnominal initials include, but are not limited to, those in the following list:

ACNP	Acute Care Nurse Practitioner
ANP	Adult Nurse Practitioner
APN	Advanced Practice Nurse (refers to the four recognized general areas of advanced professional specialization: CNM, CNS, CRNA, and NP)
APRN	Advanced Practice Registered Nurse (same as APN)
ARNP	Advanced Registered Nurse Practitioner (refers to NPs in some US states)
CNM	Certified Nurse Midwife
CNS	Clinical Nurse Specialist
CRNA	Certified Registered Nurse Anesthetist
CRNP	Certified Registered Nurse Practitioner
CS	Clinical Specialist
DNP	Doctor of Nursing Practice (the terminal professional degree for APNs)
FNP	Family Nurse Practitioner
GNP	Gerontological Nurse Practitioner
NNP	Neonatal Nurse Practitioner
NP	Nurse Practitioner
ONP	Oncology Nurse Practitioner
PMHCNS	Psychiatric and Mental Health Clinical Nurse Specialist
PMHNP	Psychiatric and Mental Health Nurse Practitioner

PNP	Pediatric Nurse Practitioner
PsyNP	Psychiatric Nurse Practitioner
WHNP	Women's Health Nurse Practitioner

Nurses

Probably no single title in the hospital setting is as encompassing and variable when it comes to training and education as "nurse." Yet you will undoubtedly encounter nurses more frequently than anyone else in a clinical setting. There are many different variations, and the roles and responsibilities depend on what kinds of initials follow the nurse's name. These initials and the scope of practice are some of the most confusing and variable, depending on a state and hospital's rules. I recommend that you look at the initials on the nurse's identification badge. In the interest of self-empowerment, feel free to ask what sort of nurse someone is when he or she arrives, in case it's not readily apparent. Sound complex? It is, but I will try to help you make some sense of it.

A nurse may be a licensed vocational or licensed practice nurse (LVN or LPN), a registered nurse (RN), or a holder of a BSN, an MSN*, or a PhD.

LICENSED VOCATIONAL OR LICENSED PRACTICE NURSES

LVN or LPN is a title granted after completion of a nine-month program for full-time/daytime students. LVN training programs involve one educational year at a hospital, vocational technical school, or community college. After taking this training, the candidate is eligible for licensure as an LPN or LVN. These are simple nomenclature differences, depending on the state of residence. Upon completing the program, the nurse must meet the rest of the state licensing requirements, which include an examination, the National Council Licensure Examination (NCLEX). For LPNs or LVNs the examination is called the NCLEX-PN. LVNs will then be qualified to work at a hospital, but their responsibilities are lim-

---

*A nurse practitioner will hold an MSN, but an MSN does not necessarily mean the individual is a nurse practitioner.

ited, and they must work under the guidance and direction of a registered nurse.

REGISTERED NURSES

Different states have differing requirements for training and licensure of nursing. States rely on their state boards of nursing to set the regulations and educational requirements for a candidate and establish criteria for approval of training programs. I will offer some generalities, but you should check the rules in your state so that you know the credentials, capability, and privileges of the nurses in your state. For most registered nurses the training progression is as follows. They graduate from high school or obtain a GED and apply to a nursing program. There are three customary ways for an individual to be licensed as an RN: a hospital diploma program (three years), an associate's degree in nursing program (two years), or a bachelor's degree in nursing program (four years). In general, individuals must maintain a grade-point average of at least 2.0 out of 4.0.

Upon completing the program, the nurse must meet the rest of the state licensing requirements, which include an examination, the NCLEX. For RNs the examination is the NCLEX-RN.

Paramedics

If your entry into the healthcare system involves calling an ambulance, then the first provider you will encounter will be either a paramedic and/ or an EMT. The term "medic" is often used interchangeably between paramedics and EMTs. Here is a little help to know who you are dealing with.

Both EMTs and paramedics are *certified* healthcare providers who are trained to treat and transport victims of emergencies. Their certification differs from conventional licensure, as the certificates are generally more vocational or technical credentials. Although some states offer "licenses" for paramedics, it still is not meant to imply a professional license or autonomy of practice. All EMTs and paramedics operate under the authorization of a physician medical director. Basically, this means that the physician is providing assurances to the public about the competence of the medic and is authorized by his or her medical license, that is, the medic is working as an extension of the medical director's medical license. A paramedic and an EMT cannot function or administer care without a medical director (physician) who guarantees the capability and quality of the medic treating a patient. State emergency medical services (EMS) divisions or departments regulate the requirements and credentials of medics. Medic certification varies greatly from state to state. The EMS division oversees testing and validation of training programs and acts on complaints. If there is justification, it may revoke the medic's certification. These divisions are often a part of the state's health department. Today many states require an examination administered by the National Registry of Emergency Medical Technicians (NREMT).

EMTs provide basic life support to victims. Skills include immobilization and splinting, bandaging, administering oxygen and medications, cardiopulmonary resuscitation, defibrillation, extrication, and airway management. EMTs may work in an emergency department, fire department, public-gathering venues (like racetracks), and industrial settings. Primarily, though, the certification is aimed at providing care in an ambulance. EMTs and paramedics work under very specific, written protocols provided by a medical director. These protocols are symptom-driven algorithms addressing life-threatening problems.

Medics may utilize *offline* medical direction, which means the medic refers to the written book of protocols, and *online* direction, which means they speak directly to the physician medical director via radio or telephone.

For most medics the training progression is as follows. They graduate from high school or obtain a GED, although some EMT "basics" may begin via a high school–level program. The biggest differences between paramedics and EMTs are the training and scope of practice (what they are allowed to do). Basic EMTs usually receive 120–150 hours of training, while paramedics get anywhere from 1,200 to 1,800 hours of training. Paramedic programs often award two-year associate's degrees. There has been a recent trend among educators toward "fast tracking," or compressing the medic training from a year down to six months, but these programs are not common.

Administrators

These are the executives, the "suits." They are the businesspeople of the healthcare industry. Just like executives in any other area, their primary interest and concern is the efficient and profitable running of a business that delivers health care. As in other corporations they may carry the title of "manager," "director," or "officer." Think chief operating officer, chief executive officer, or director.

This is quite distinct from the title "medical director," which indicates that the individual is a clinically trained healthcare professional focused primarily on delivery of medical or health care. For a medical director, the business is generally a secondary consideration. At least, ideally it is.

Administrative health services managers, also called healthcare executives or healthcare administrators, plan, direct, and coordinate medical and healthcare systems. They might manage an entire facility or specialize in managing a specific type of clinical area or department, or manage the business of a medical practice for a group of physicians. This is a critical position in the system, and when you as a patient interact with the administrator or an administrative person, you should realize that this individual will be less able to specifically address a clinical or clinically related issue and will be more interested in and familiar with the service delivery issues. Just so you know, from a customer satisfaction standpoint, this person is likely to be the most influential. Like the owner of a business, the administrator is concerned with your service and satisfaction. A medical or nursing director hopefully and appropriately will care about that, but to a lesser extent than whether the medical providers diagnosed you correctly or saved your life. You should be happy about that.

So, a medical or nursing director has to be a physician or a nurse. An administrator or executive can be a physician or nurse but does not have to be. For most administrators the educational progression is as follows: they have a high school diploma or GED, they have completed college and hold a bachelor's degree, and some go on to a master's degree or doctorate, generally with an emphasis on business.

As health care changes, medical and health service managers must be able to adapt to changes in laws, regulations, and technology geared toward the efficient and profitable running of a system. This requires the same professional approach as one expects in a clinician. As mentioned earlier, ideally the administrators interface in a manner that is complementary and supportive to those providing your care, so it is the best it can be.

Licensure versus Certification

This is a pretty confounding set of credentials, yet the terminology is thrown about from provider to provider with little explanation. They do not mean the same thing. In reality, the two words and what they mean can be nonsensical and bewildering. The truth is that certification or licensure may mean autonomy and privilege when applied to one type of healthcare player and mean something very different when applied to another. They may even have different meanings when applied to the same category or type of provider, depending on their location. Confused? You should be.

Here are some examples. A surgeon, in order to practice, must be a licensed physician. It is a state credential indicating that certain "steps" in training and testing have been completed in accordance with a state's law. A surgeon generally will also be board certified, meaning that the surgeon has completed a program and set of validations established by the specialty the individual intends to practice. So a surgeon must be licensed to be legal and board certified to be in good standing with the specialty association.

In general this is how the two "credentials" apply, though there are many exceptions. For example, a paramedic must have certification in order to work as a paramedic. As has been stated earlier, some states also have licensure, though neither credential allows autonomy of practice. (Both certified and licensed medics must have a medical director's authorization to touch you.)

So, I wish I could offer an easier answer, but once again, check with your local and state laws or legal/statutory bodies. They will explain, in detail, what those words mean depending on the type of care provider. A state or local health department is often a good place to start.

Table 2: Some Generalities about Medical Training

Title	High school	College	Training	Advanced training	Advanced training	Advanced training
MD/DO	Mandatory	4 years: bachelor's degree with prerequisites (mandatory)	4 years medical school resulting in doctor of medicine (mandatory)	Internship (mandatory), 1 year	Residency specialty training (most have this), 3–5 years	Fellowship specialty (some have this), 1–3 years
PA	Mandatory	4 years: bachelor's degree with prerequisites (mandatory)	3 years of PA school resulting in a PA or PA/MSN	Specialty training (varies), 1–3 years	No	No
APN	Mandatory	4 years: bachelor's degree in nursing	Master's degree, 2–2.5 years; CRNA, midwife, and general (some may require one prior year of work experience)	No	No	No
RN	Yes	Varies: diploma, 3 years; associate's degree, 2 years; BSN, 4 years	No	No	No	No
LVN	Yes	Vocational, 1 year	No	No	No	No
Paramedic	Yes	Vocational/non-degreed, usually 1,300 hours; varies greatly	No	No	No	No
EMT-Basic	Yes	Vocational, 120 hours; varies	No	No	No	No

Without a doubt I have not covered all of the players you may encounter in a hospital, but you get an idea of the variability and scope of practice of some of the more commonly seen members of a healthcare team. Physicians are autonomous. The other healthcare professionals have supervisory arrangements that can vary substantially. Paraprofessionals or technicians can function only with strictly defined supervision. The take-home message is that if you encounter someone who is about to administer a medication, puncture your skin, or otherwise apply some modality and you don't know exactly who or what kind of medical practitioner the person is, *Ask!*

You have every right to know who the people are that you encounter, and what they are allowed to do and why. Given the potential impact of their actions on your health, you would be well advised to find out. If someone appears offended or is reluctant to disclose his or her training experience and background, do not accept that. You are not helpless. Your consent is required for anything that anyone plans to do to you, and it can be withdrawn at any time, by you! It's like a vampire wanting to enter your house—and if you have had your blood drawn, you know what I mean—but can't do it without your invitation. That is a power that you possess. Exercise it.

The above table is a quick "go-to" tool that you should keep close at hand so you can keep track of the players.

CHAPTER 3

AMBULANCES

YOU WANNA GO
WHERE EVERYBODY
KNOWS YOUR NUMBER

I n the United States it's a pretty good bet that almost all of us have a somewhat similar expectation when we say, "Get me an ambulance" or "Call 911." It's almost like someone saying "I'm in love!" We all recognize the words and what they mean in concept, but the differences in each mind are as unique as the person speaking and the person hearing that phrase.

So it is probably useful to start off with a couple of assumptions. The way you enter the healthcare system will have a lot to do with how you are treated, how quickly you are treated, how your medical problem is perceived, and how you will perceive the situation.

If your physician or healthcare provider determines that you need a procedure or further evaluation (X-ray, CT scan, MRI, or the dreaded, intrusive 'scoping) after an examination, he or she will likely facilitate the arrangements, and the pace and pressure will be less. Communication and dialogue will be generally optimal, and the experience will be more to your control and liking.

If your physician or another healthcare provider determines you are teetering on the yawning maw of death and need emergency care within the next minutes or hours, he or she may call an ambulance, and the pace and pressure of the situation will be very different. Communication and dialogue may be hurried and/or nonexistent, and the experience will be less in your control and probably less enjoyable.

Now—and bear with me on this—let's pretend you have a pet wolverine, ignoring the multiple issues that indicates about judgment. Let's then suppose you are out walking your pet wolverine so he can get some exercise. You stroll past the hospital and a car backfires, frightening your pet wolverine, who is normally very easygoing. Your wolverine reacts badly, and the result leaves you with a need and a desire to alter the planned walk and head on in to the emergency department (ED) at the hospital. Your physician or healthcare provider's involvement will be a secondary consideration. Chances are the pace and pressure of the moment will be a lot more accelerated and dynamic, and communication and dialogue with the triage nurse in the ED will probably be much more hurried and direct. (Triage is the process for sorting injured people into groups based on their need for or likely benefit from immediate medical treatment.) The experience will be less in your control and, I'm betting, less enjoyable.

Now, if you are at home giving your pet wolverine a bath in the tub and he is having a bad day and acts accordingly, you may be calling 911 or accessing the system through an emergency dispatcher, and your physician or healthcare provider will not be a part of the conversation at all. The pace and pressure will definitely be accelerated and different—and I am going out on a limb here—but I would guess it won't be in your control at all and will probably be a whole lot less enjoyable for a bunch of reasons.

So let's imagine the conversation goes like this:

> 911 Operator: This is 911. Do you need fire, police, or ambulance?
> You: I need an ambulance.
> 911 Operator: Stay on the line. I am transferring you to EMS.

Most people have a pretty good idea about what EMS is. It's the ambulance service that provides municipal emergency medical transport and associated treatment while en route to the hospital. That is exactly correct yet incredibly nonspecific. And it matters.

EMS came into existence in the United States during the Civil War, when extraordinary numbers of combat casualties in the aftermath of battle required transport to field hospitals. It has carried over to the modern era of domestic accident and illness response with significantly different outlays every decade or so. Over the last 30 years, EMS has transformed from a patient-retrieval service operated by funeral homes and staffed by inadequately trained crews, to advanced, out-of-hospital healthcare providers, with commensurate stabilizing medications and medical equipment brought to the patient.

The education and knowledge expected from EMS have increased greatly as the concept of prehospital patient care has evolved. To keep pace with this expectation, emergency medical responders and their medical directors must keep abreast of the most current and acceptable treatments used in hospitals. Even as late as the early 1960s, EMS was not always viewed as a component of the healthcare system but rather as a transport method comparable to the crude system used in the Civil War 100 years earlier.

After the passage of the Highway Traffic Safety Act and the publication of *Accidental Death and Disability: The Neglected Disease of Modern Society*, written by a commission representing the National Academy of Sciences, National Research Council, and Division of Medical Services in 1966, the Department of Transportation–National Highway Traffic Safety Administration (DOT–NHTSA) was assigned responsibility for and oversight of guideline development related to the provision of EMS.

These efforts included the first attempt at standardizing curriculum development and designing standards for ambulances and communications systems. The prehospital transportation system received an additional boost in 1970 when the Department of Defense combined resources with DOT and the Department of Health, Education, and Welfare (HEW), the precursor to the Department of Health and Human Services (DHHS), to create the Military Assistance to Safety and Traffic (MAST) program.

Following lessons learned during military actions in Vietnam, it was decided that the use of air resources to extricate seriously injured patients from crash sites to appropriate medical facilities would allow the greatest opportunity for survival because of reduced transport times.

The 1980s were a period of growth and standardization for EMS, especially regarding patient-care techniques and training. Advances in the treatment of the cardiac patient hit the scene, and EMS was thrust into new standards of care for cardiac patients. Cardiopulmonary resuscitation (CPR) became the focus of a new public education drive, and the American Heart Association (AHA) came out with an Advanced Cardiac Life Support (ACLS) course that increased the impact that prehospital personnel could have on cardiac patients. Through these and many other changes, EMS was identified as an integral partner in the healthcare industry. Members of local government and the medical profession were called on to assume leadership and lay the groundwork for standardized, unified prehospital systems.

If you thought the different credentialing discussions about healthcare providers were intricate, confusing, and extremely variable, hold on to your hats when it comes to EMS. Often the term "ambulance" and EMS are used interchangeably. In fact, EMS is the "service" of responding in the prehospital setting and providing early and transitory stabilizing care. The ambulance is generally the vehicle operated by EMS personnel (EMT, paramedic, or others) used to carry the injured or ill person.

Not all things EMS are related to transport though. Such situations as medical aid stations or attendance and "stand by" at big gatherings (the Super Bowl, World Series, etc.) still constitute EMS, even though they are in a slightly different mission configuration. They may also use non-traditional conveyance, such as configured golf carts and bicycles with "jump bags" full of basic medical supplies, or first-aid stations with no conveyance.

EMS provider licenses are different from paramedic licensure mentioned earlier and are generally state and sometimes community issuances. This type of licensure refers to the "business" license of the ambulance provider or "company." This licensing process includes inspection and review of the medical protocols for treatment, the formulary (or medical material supply list) and the presence of such material on the ambulance, "medic" credentials, and the mechanical maintenance of ambulances.

For training, the medic curriculum, Emergency Medical Technician-Basic (EMT-B): National Standard Curriculum, is the cornerstone of EMS prehospital training. The EMT-Paramedic (EMT-P): National Standard Curriculum represents the minimum required information to be presented within a course leading to certification as a paramedic. It is recognized that there is additional specific education that will be required of paramedics who operate in the field, such as ambulance driving, heavy and light rescue, basic extrication, special needs care, individual care modalities determined by the medical director, and so on. It is also recognized that this information might differ from locality to locality and that each training program or system should identify and provide special instruction for these training requirements. This curriculum is intended to prepare a medically competent paramedic to operate in the field.

According to the National Highway Transportation Safety Authority (NHTSA),

Emergency medical service is widely regarded as including the full spectrum of emergency care from recognition of the emergency, telephone access of the system, provision of prehospital care, through definitive care in the hospital. It often also includes medical response to disasters, planning for and provision of medical coverage at mass gatherings, and interfacility transfers of patients. However, for the purposes of this document, the definition of EMS is limited to the more traditional, colloquial meaning: prehospital health care for patients with real or perceived emergencies from the time point of emergency telephone access until arrival and transfer of care to the hospital.

Earlier I touched on the training and credentialing of EMTs and paramedics. The level of credential of the medic, the treatment and medications authorized by the medical director, and the material on the ambulance constitute another classification of ambulances: whether they are Advanced Life Support capable or Basic Life Support capable.

Medical Direction

According to NHTSA, medical direction is an essential component of prehospital training and thus is included in the EMT-B curriculum. This physician involvement should be in place for all aspects of EMS training programs, specifically for every ambulance service/rescue squad. Online and/or offline medical direction must be established and in place to allow for personnel to carry out and assist with the administration of medications to patients. The position of medical director in an organization can be quite complex. Medical directors may be employees of the ambulance company or the municipal entity (city or county), or they may be contracted to provide direction. They have a great deal of responsibility for the care the medic provides. The medical director must also keep track of the credentials of the medic because any care provided is an extension of the medical director's authorization. This is an interesting relationship between the medical director and the individual medic. It's a lot like the medical director is vouching for the medic whenever he or she provides care.

As mentioned earlier, the state provides the certification of the medic, but the medic must have the medical director's authorization to render care. Without it the medic cannot legally do so. Therefore, every EMS must have a medical director.

Quality improvement is also a required component of the medical director's contribution to EMS operation. As you can see, the role of medical direction is paramount in assuring the provision of highest-quality prehospital care. Medical directors should work with individual personnel and systems to review prehospital cases and strive to achieve a sound method of continuous quality improvement. The medical director is also a key determinant of the care you will receive in an ambulance.

EMS Medical Director

A licensed physician who provides the following services for an ambulance service or EMS system:

- Offline medical direction in the form of written, symptom- or diagnosis-driven medical treatment protocols that medics must follow in treating you
- Online medical direction, which amounts to real-time active discussion and consultation that medics must follow in treating you
- Responsibility for the performance of the medics, review of performance, compliance with the protocols, and the appropriateness and effectiveness of treatment provided
- Maintenance of protocols and treatment that is consistent with the accepted standard of care
- Case review of medic care
- Setting standards for educational remediation and continuing education for medics
- Authorization of medics—that is, the medics are acting with the provision, endorsement, and as extensions of the medical director and the director's clinical responsibility— often described by medics as working "under the doctor's license"
- Advising business and operational directors of EMS on specifics of their performance that would enhance or avoid obstruction of proper medical care

Advanced versus Basic Life Support Units

What is being offered here is again a generalization. Individual states and some communities or municipalities offer language differences that identify the type or "level" of care that is provided on an ambulance. This terminology is often written on the ambulance. You might see the letters BLS, meaning Basic Life Support; ALS, meaning Advanced Life Support; or even MICU, meaning Mobile Intensive Care Unit. In some areas ALS and MICU mean approximately the same thing, so for purposes of generality I will restrain myself to the difference in care between ALS and BLS.

The main difference has to do with the distinctions of the level of care delivered based on the credential level of the medics on the ambulance and the material resources (the drugs). Remember that the protocols provided by the medical director determine the specific level of care. The level also relates to the medical tools and instruments (the monitors and defibrillators) in the ambulance inventory that medics can use to attempt stabilization on the way to the hospital. So, think drugs and defibrillators when you see ALS instead of BLS!

The AHA offers regularly updated guidelines to assist in the emergent treatment of cardiac issues. It utilizes expert reviewers and research addressing cardiovascular care to create the guidelines for care and publish them accordingly. It also classifies the care based on basic modalities like BLS (CPR, AED [automated external defibrillator] use) and advanced methods like ALS (intravenous drug administration, artificial breathing and oxygen, and defibrillation). Again, a very broad generalization here, but the main difference in whether something is advanced or basic has to do with puncturing skin, inserting tubes, and administering drugs. BLS doesn't generally include insertion of needles, cutting the skin, or inserting things in the body, and it doesn't generally involve the administration of medications or drugs.

Staffing

Ambulances that are ALS capable generally have a paramedic onboard and the medications and IV apparatus (along with some advanced breathing-tube applications) that allow paramedics to function commensurate with

their training and credentials, and the medical director's authorization, as described in their protocols. BLS-capable ambulances usually do not.

There are a variety of other applications and combinations, such as helicopter ambulances, the previously described specialized EMS, military and law enforcement medical support, and mobile pediatric ICUs, but again these are the basics.

In short, this is a classification that matters to you as a patient, and whether you get the appropriate ambulance and crew response or not can often be influenced by how and what you say to the 911 dispatcher. So let's get back to our EMS call resulting from the pet wolverine attack.

The 911 call taker has transferred you to the EMS dispatcher. This person is extremely important. This is a trained person who will ask specific questions to determine the correct type of ambulance (ALS or BLS) you need. He or she may also make some recommendations to you regarding what to do until the ambulance arrives. He or she will communicate your information, in emergency response–specific language, to the EMS crew, telling them how emergent the situation is and what they should prepare for when they arrive. All this can make a big difference in your outcome and care. Dispatchers work from standardized protocols, called EMD protocols, to assist their decision making. So here is how this conversation might go.

> EMS Dispatcher: EMS, what is your emergency?
> You: My pet wolverine, Ramon, just bit me.
> EMS Dispatcher: Uhhhh . . . is the wolverine still running around, or is it still a threat?
> You: No. Ramon is having a time out in his kennel.
> EMS Dispatcher: Okay. Good. Where did he bite you?
> You: On my leg.
> EMS Dispatcher: Are you bleeding?

Phones and Emergencies

Cell phones and landlines differ greatly in regard to tracing or identifying your location. If you have a landline or "hard" line, emergency services *may* be able to reconnect. Cellular or wireless phones are less exact, though it varies. Bottom line, Emergency Services can call back, but the ability to trace and locate may not be as reliable, so *Don't hang up!*

Also, ask your local fire department—*call the nonemergency number*— about this before you have an issue. Be informed.

And so on . . . The dispatcher is likely to ask other questions: How much blood have you lost? Is the bleeding bright red or dark? Is it spurting? And dispatchers will always, and I mean always, want you to stay on the line until they say the call is over. This may mean staying on until the ambulance arrives.

Notice that the EMS dispatcher's first questions had to do with determining if things were going on that made the scene still dangerous. This is important, because the dispatcher will need to determine, if beyond EMS, other supporting emergency services like the police department, animal control, a hazardous materials team (HAZMAT), and others also need to respond. So telling him or her that Ramon was in his kennel was invaluable. The dispatcher then focused on medical care and assessment questions in order to better advise you until the ambulance arrives.

Earlier I discussed how medical people communicate, how they think. Knowing this and being organized and direct in how you relate your issues are important in helping them help you.

WHAT YOU CAN DO

- Be as organized in describing what happened as possible. Write some notes down if you can.
- Be prepared to answer questions.
- Remain calm. This is hard, but it is huge in making sure you get the best help possible.
- Tell medical responders everything truthfully.
- If you have any medical conditions, tell them. Sometimes chronic medical conditions, medications, social or illicit drugs, and smoking and drinking can make a big difference in the type of medications you can receive in the ambulance without risk.

As stated earlier, ambulances are also characterized by mechanical configuration or design (a truck or van chassis). This diagram illustrates what you might realistically expect to show up. The differences are how the "box" (square compartment where the medical care takes place) is configured and what kind of chassis the unit uses.

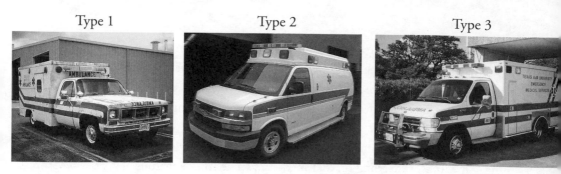

A Type 1 ambulance is a "box" mounted onto a truck chassis.*

A Type 2 ambulance is built into a van-type chassis. The only major modification to the vehicle is that the roof is raised. Type 2 ambulances are used mostly for interhospital transfers and are rarely used as EMS vehicles.

A Type 3 ambulance is a "box" mounted onto a van chassis.

This sort of distinction and categorization is really not so much a patient-care concern or consideration, but it is part of the language used and you do want to be informed. For a potential patient there are two more distinctions: clinical care classification and the municipal-versus-private classification. So let's talk about whether your service is municipal or private.

Municipal versus Private Service

Generally, when a person dials 911 and an ambulance arrives, the expectation is that the ambulance is a part of the municipal system, a local department. That is not always the case. Your 911 EMS provider may be a part of the local fire department, an independent municipal agency, or a private ambulance company that is contracted to provide the service to the local jurisdiction.

The provision of 911 EMS is a service established by local legal statute. So it is created by a legal authority. How that is established varies according to whether the authority comes from a state law, a county board or

*The ambulance that shows up in response to your pet wolverine bite will probably be a Type 1 or 3.

governing body, or a municipal law. This is something you will want to know, and the time to learn that is before you need help. In any case the "authority having jurisdiction" (AHJ) has various options for providing ambulances. AHJ refers to an organization, office, or individual responsible for enforcing the requirement of a code or standard, or for approving equipment, materials, an installation, or a procedure.

The AHJ can directly purchase and run ambulances through an emergency agency or through an agency like the fire department or hospital system, or it can contract the service from a private company. If it is a direct provision, or through an agency or department, the ambulance will declare that on the side of the box. For some reason, it always seems to be in big reflective letters! If the service is a contract ambulance, it will have the company's name on the side of the box.

Why do you care? If you have a positive experience or a problem, it is important to know how to direct your compliment or complaint. It also matters when you receive a bill. Most people believe that the fire department or EMS authority is publicly funded by taxes. It is, but EMS in many states and municipalities can also charge the patient (you) additionally for each response or call. So support for EMS is by both a tax base and direct billing. The price can also vary widely. In some cities, EMS calls cost more than $1,000.

Paid and Volunteer Services

Some services, especially in underserved or rural areas, may be provided by paid, volunteer, or combination staff, often for economic reasons or because the availability of staffing personnel is limited. In general, paid staff are on shift and in a station awaiting a call when not responding. Theoretically, this should make their response times quicker and more predictable. Volunteer staffing is cheaper for a jurisdiction, as the staff are not paid, but they may have to report from home before initiating a response. This may or may not affect response time. Similarly, the location and number of stations in an area and their proximity will influence how quickly the ambulance gets to you.

What Should You Ask before You Need 911 Support?

- Municipal or private contractor?
- Average response time for your address and area?
- Paid or volunteer service?
- ALS or BLS or combination?
- How do they determine level of call and what level to send?
- Who is the operations director or chief?
- Who is the medical director?

When the Ambulance Arrives

The responding crew will need information. The more you can provide in an organized format, the quicker they will be able to react in caring for you and the better the care will be. On the next page is a sign that could be placed in your front window or somewhere obvious as EMS arrives in your driveway to let them know that your medical information is readily available in an organized and orderly format. There is also a medical information chart that you can fill out in advance for EMS, but certainly whatever format you use should include all of the information described, and its location should be consistent with what you put on the window signage.

So EMS has arrived. They have *packaged* you, meaning you are secured to a stretcher after being medically assessed. Then any stabilizing procedures (like an intravenous line) are performed, and you are taken to the hospital where you are seen in the emergency department. A quick word about that: A lot of people will tell you that it does not matter, but the fact is that arrival at an ED by EMS is addressed differently than arriving by a "personally operated vehicle," or POV (your car). For one thing, the crew has to get the ambulance unloaded and "back in service." That means, at the very least, you *have* to be assessed by a triage nurse or physician, thus transferring your care. The ED staff may still send you to the waiting area instead of placing you in a bed, but you will at least get initial attention.

And now, back to your wolverine attack . . . So the ambulance has arrived. They have packaged you. You are in the back of the ambulance or "in the box." They will have knowledge of the local hospitals and the capability of each respective hospital in dealing with your particular type of problem.

Capability and Availability

These two words are very important. *Capability* refers to the sophistication of care a facility can provide. Think trauma, cardiac care, stroke care, surgical and intensive unit, and specialty problems.

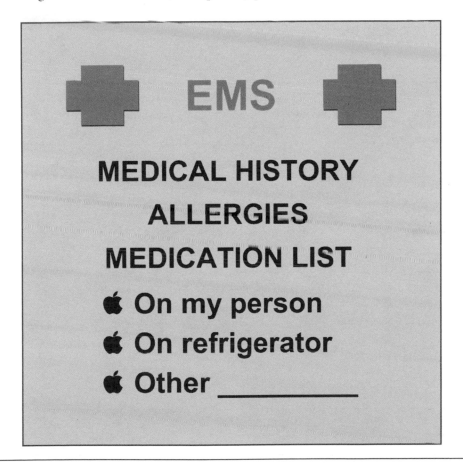

Medical Information Chart

Last name:	First name:	Date completed:

Emergency Contact Information

Name:	Relationship:	Phone number:

Personal Information

Date of birth:	Age:	☐ Male ☐ Female	Social Security number:
Height:	Weight:	Blood type :	Last tetanus booster:	Last TB test:

Medical History   Please check all that apply. ☐ No Medical Problems

☐ High blood pressure	☐ Diabetes	☐ Seizures	☐ Asthma	☐ Heart attack	☐ Stroke
☐ Broken bones	☐ Arthritis	☐ Cancer	☐ Heart disease	☐ Migraines	☐ Back problems

☐ Other:

Allergies

☐ No known drug allergies   ☐ YES SEE BELOW

☐ Other: Please list _____

Your Prescribed Medications (List all medications you are currently taking as well as the strength and frequency you take them.)

	Medication name	Strength	Quantity/day	What medication is for	Doctor's name
1					
2					
3					
4					
5					

Social History

Smoke tobacco	Chew tobacco	Alcohol

Physician Information

Name:	City/State:	Phone number:

Abuse of the System

EMS performed well is a wonderful thing. It is really the community and civil service working at its best. That said, it also requires that a responsible community use it only when it is necessary. It's not an expensive taxi with a license to break the speed limit and should not be treated that way. On the other hand, if you are uncertain as to whether you really need EMS, do *not* hesitate to call 911. The benefit will go beyond the initial "call" by the ambulance. It will extend to your treatment in the ED and the rest of your hospital stay, if that is necessary.

Availability is a dynamic issue related to real-time overtasking of a hospital. In other words, is it full or maxed out? In some cases, hospitals may go on *diversion* status, meaning they are putting EMS on notice that they really cannot provide the level of care normally expected because they are at full capacity or are overwhelmed by increased numbers of patients. Ambulances will, via the dispatcher, attempt to take patients to other hospitals during this period.

Against Medical Advice

The phrase "against medical advice" (AMA) is a fairly common consideration in care, not just with ambulances and 911. This also occurs in EDs and hospitals. It's a special situation that arises when a patient (you) disagrees with the recommendation or advice given by a medical provider. In the case of EMS, if you decline transportation to a hospital in the ambulance, you may be asked to sign a document acknowledging that the attendants are recommending you go with them in the interest of your safety or because of the severity of your injuries or illness or potential injuries or illness. Your signature makes it clear that you have been counseled about the risks and that you are nevertheless declining. It's not just a clinical tool. It is also a legal tool providing protection for the EMS service or the healthcare institution and providers with whom you are disagreeing about the disposition of your care. If you are being asked to sign an AMA form, make sure that you clearly understand what treatment course is being recommended by the providers and why. Make sure you really are in disagreement with what they are suggesting and that the risks of such a decision are understood. In the aftermath of some injuries or when an illness that could affect judgment is occurring, you should not be asked to sign this "contract."

Where You Gonna Go?

Determination of destination is another complex issue. This varies a lot and is an issue of state and local law. In some states, a patient can dictate or request a hospital destination. In others, the patient does not have that option. The destination is determined by the 911 service. If your locale allows you to have a say in the destination, then knowing your local hospitals' capabilities becomes even more important. So, check your local laws and your local service in advance.

And now back to your fictional injury . . . Once you are packaged and en route to the hospital, the medics will call in to the ED saying they are on the way and provide the following information:

- The nature of your problem (a wolverine bite)
- The severity of your problem
- The "traffic" or urgency with which they are driving (whether they will drive with emergency lights and sirens running or not)
- The estimated time of arrival

This information provided before your arrival allows the ED staff to prepare and/or advise or suggest care that the ambulance attendants should provide. (The medical director generally makes those decisions otherwise.)

Whether you arrive by ambulance or POV, you can expect that you will be seen and evaluated in the ED. The justification and law supporting this assurance is called the Emergency Medical Treatment and Active Labor Act (EMTALA). EMTALA was passed in 1986 as part of the Consolidated Omnibus Budget Reconciliation Act (COBRA). It requires hospitals to provide care to anyone needing *emergency* medical treatment regardless of citizenship, legal status, or ability to pay. In fact, there are no reimbursement provisions at all. Hospitals may only transfer or discharge patients needing emergency treatment under their own informed consent, after stabilization, or when their condition requires transfer to a hospital better equipped to administer the treatment.

EMTALA applies to "participating hospitals." The statute defines "participating hospitals" as those that accept payment from the Department of Health and Human Services, Centers for Medicare and Medicaid Services (CMS) under the Medicare program. However, in practical terms, EMTALA applies to virtually all hospitals in the United States, with the exception of the Shriners Hospitals for Children, Indian Health Service hospitals, and Veterans Affairs hospitals, and all patients, not just Medicare and Medicaid patients.

EMTALA does not mean that a hospital has to accept you in transfer from another hospital, so getting to the proper facility initially is pretty important.

Back to your injury . . . The ambulance has taken you to the hospital, and you have been evaluated and transferred from the gurney to a bed. The ambulance crew has left to "return to service." Remember that while they were transporting you and at the hospital, they were "out of service," meaning they could not respond to care in their normal area, which could affect response times to other people in distress. During this time other ambulances in adjacent areas would have had to respond to your ambulance crew's normal calls. This can really negatively affect response time. If enough simultaneous calls are occurring, then a condition of "mutual aid" may be initiated in which neighboring jurisdictions may provide temporary coverage for calls. In that case, response times can be quite lengthy.

Now it turns out, let's say, that a small blood vessel and a tendon in your leg are injured that will require you to be transferred to another hospital where proper surgical support is available. An agreement must be reached between the potential accepting hospital and the one in which you are currently waiting. The potentially accepting hospital is not required to accept you, but generally the ethical compulsion to provide care and your ability to pay will be in your favor.

Once this agreement has taken place, you will be transported to the new facility, but the "unit" carrying you will probably not be a 911 provider. In most cases a private ambulance will be utilized. This is a strictly for-profit healthcare business service and not affiliated with the emergency response that brought you to the hospital. It still is required that proper support and care be provided by the statutory authority, and "lights and sirens" may be employed if you "medically decompensate" or become unstable medically during the transport, but it is generally a much more conventional and calm transport mechanism.

And on that note, a word about money. Remember what I said earlier? Most people believe that their taxes pay for the 911/EMS ambulance service. Most people are shocked when during their convalescence they receive a bill for the 911/EMS transport to the hospital. A patient who was recovering at home from a heart attack once told me that the bill he received almost made him have to call 911 again.

So which is actually correct? Do taxes pay for the service, or can they bill you? Well, both. Your taxes go toward the creation and subsidization of EMS and all emergency services, such as the EMS or fire stations whose names you see on the trucks and boxes described earlier. In many jurisdictions, EMS is also allowed to bill for individual services. What is allowable and what is not are very locale specific. So, to use a Latin phrase (remember Latin is the language of US medicine), *caveat emptor*, or "let the buyer beware"! Research this in advance, and be prepared for some moderate sticker shock.

One note of admonition, though. You should not hesitate to access or call 911 over a concern for cost. The bill that is sent is one that can be negotiated and paid over time, and you can't be refused care due to finances.

So, you are "loaded" into the private ambulance and carried to the new hospital—hopefully not Our Lady of Perpetual Confusion Hospital System—much wiser about the system, EMS, and how prehospital care works. In the next chapter we explore the similar complexities of hospitals, how they are classified, and how you can be better empowered should you need to be admitted.

Oh, and one last thing. The next time you are choosing a pet, maybe you should consider a goldfish.

CHAPTER 4

HOSPITALS

WHAT YOU REALLY NEED TO KNOW
BEFORE YOU GOTTA GO

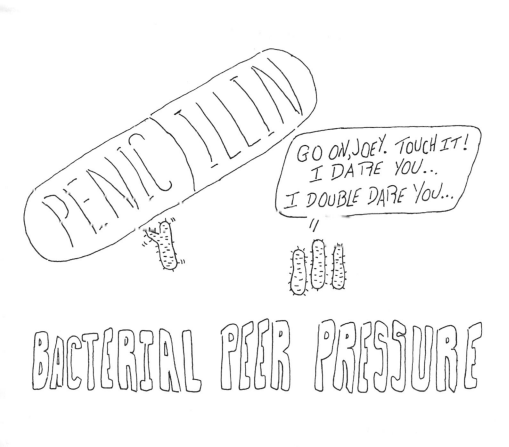

OHHH MANNN... NOT THIS THING AGAIN

I n the last chapter we used the fictional depiction of a pet wolverine attack to describe the access and particulars of the prehospital care system. As important as it is to know how and when to use EMS to your greatest and most efficient advantage, it is at the hospital that the definitive work of addressing a medical problem occurs.

Earlier I referenced the Our Lady of Perpetual Confusion Hospital System. As absurd as it sounds, perpetual confusion is what is in store if you are not prepared for the intricacies and nuances of care at the hospital. Frankly, if you are not prepared in advance, you may not even end up in the right kind of hospital. You might end up at Cedars of Frustration or Acme Medical Center, and the specific kind of care needed may not be as readily available at OLPCHS. At the very least, you may be in for a transfer with a variable timetable. At worst, it can be a critical mistake.

It is an odd state of affairs that regarding active consumerism—buying a car, cat toys, or gardening equipment or booking a hotel—most people put more effort into researching the product than they do in evaluating their local hospitals. When you consider what might be at stake, this seems not only ironic and potentially dangerous but downright crazy.

This chapter describes how to research your local hospitals and how to know what to ask before you have to enter OLPCHS either by ambulance or under your own steam and what the answers really mean. As you may have noticed in the previous chapters, there is a great deal of variability among titles, organization, and accountability because of the number of players in the healthcare system. This is also true regarding hospitals.

Most people think of hospitals when they are contemplating emergency care and surgical care or specialty care for conditions like cancer, pediatric illnesses, or psychiatric care. Chances are if you have a chronic illness such as a heart condition or kidney failure, then you probably already have an idea of your appropriate institution.

So let's start with emergency care. The most basic thing for you as a potential patient to know is where you may be going and the hospital's capability *in advance.* Notice that I did not use the word *capacity.* That word in health care relates to potential application of existing equipment or the ability to access a medical or surgical specialist. Capability is more immediately functional, such as when there is a specialist "in house." It matters. You'll see.

It naturally follows that the time to research this is while you are calm and well, not when you are ill and distracted by the stress of a situation. That seems like an obvious point, but it's surprising how many people don't know which hospital they want to use until they are in crisis mode. Even if they have thought about it in advance, most ask only one or two people and just go with that or do an Internet "consumer" search. While the latter is good, consumer reporting often has less to do with the validity of care and more to do with perceptions or consumer satisfaction, which ironically may have nothing at all to do with the real quality of the care provided.

In the United States, most hospitals have an emergency department that is open 24 hours a day, seven days a week, but in some rural and in some "frontier" areas, that may not be the case. This is something you will certainly want to know. So, ask.

Population Density

The definitions vary by state, but this is a generality for population density:*

- Frontier: Fewer than 6 people per square mile
- Rural: 6–19.9 people per square mile
- Densely settled rural: 20–39.9 people per square mile
- Semi-urban: 40–149.9 people per square mile
- Urban: 150 or more people per square mile

*Governor's Mental Health Services Planning Council–Rural and Frontier Subcommittee, State of Kansas

Emergency Care

TRICARE, a health care program of the US Department of Defense Military Health System, defines an emergency as "a medical, maternity, or psychiatric condition that would lead a 'prudent lay person' (someone with average knowledge of health and medicine and sound judgment) to believe that a serious medical condition exists, or that the absence of immediate medical attention would result in a threat to life, limb, or eyesight, or when the person has painful symptoms requiring immediate attention to relieve suffering." That is a long sentence, but it comes straight from a government text, and I think they were trying to save tax dollars by not printing periods.

The TRICARE passage includes situations in which a person is in severe pain or is at immediate risk to self or others. So what it really means is that the one determining if something is an emergency is you.

An emergency department, also known as accident and emergency (A&E), emergency room (ER), or casualty department, is a medical treatment facility specializing in the acute care of patients who arrive without prior appointment, either by their own means or by ambulance. An ED is usually found in a hospital or medical center with supporting surgical and intensive care support immediately available.

Again, this is speaking in general, but most emergency *departments* can do some similar things regarding fundamental stabilization. They will be able to place you on basic cardiovascular monitors, draw blood for tests (though the sophistication and speed of the test results vary greatly), establish IV access, and give medications. In four distinct and critical areas, however, they may not differ a great deal. This is really about adequate depth and immediate availability of certain resources, such as properly trained and experienced surgeons, operating room staff and equipment, anesthesiologists, intensive care units, and supportive services. These are the four areas:

- Trauma care
- Burn care
- Stroke care
- Cardiac and vascular care

Some of the most important questions as you make your inquiries *before you are ill* are the following standards or basis of the claims the hospital makes regarding trauma, burn, stroke, and cardiac care.

- The credentialing standard (the criteria)
- The body or organization used to support their claims of capability
- When they are due for reevaluation
- If they don't have all capabilities, what arrangements they have for referral and transfer, including method of transfer (helicopter or ground transport ambulance)
- Transfer times for the four categories
- Their statistics on infection rates, citations, and the number of medical mistakes as well as any awards and who gave them

The difference between an emergency department and what is sometimes called the emergency room can be very confusing. The definition of an emergency department was given earlier. Often called a "room," it is far more than just that. It's a department of the hospital. Recently, however, there have been other clinical facilities that are also called emergency rooms or use the term "urgent care center or clinic." So how do you know the difference and which one is right for you?

The language they use in describing themselves provides a big clue and often means something different depending on the person using the terminology, such as a clinician, a regulatory agency representative, or a marketing executive. If the term "center" is used rather than "clinic," there is an implied increased capability. A "center" generally implies that the facility can do more in terms of sophisticated and immediate testing or radiological evaluations.

That is not always the case, however. If the facility is freestanding— that is, not a part of an overall hospital—then it may be considered a Type B emergency department. It is not likely to be able to handle major trauma or complex or severe medical problems that might require observation or admission but may be able to address less severe issues such as these:

- Minor cuts or lacerations
- Mild to moderate asthma
- Bites (small animal or insect)
- Migraine headaches
- Vomiting without dehydration
- Rising fever

In 2007 the Centers for Medicare and Medicaid Services created the Type B emergency department designation for freestanding facilities that provide emergency care to patients. Government payments to those facilities are somewhat less than the government reimbursement for care in a hospital emergency department, but more than for an urgent care center visit. Urgent care center bills are comparable to those for visits to a primary-care doctor because urgent care centers are designed particularly for low-severity or low-acuity problems. Think of them as places to take care of medical problems when the office of your family physician or primary-care provider is not open.

Trauma is a category of medical care that varies greatly depending on the state where you live. The classification for trauma care by a hospital is generally based on its surgical and support capability. It takes into consideration the immediate or delayed access to surgeons and operating teams in order to address the unique requirements of these situations:

- Neurological or head and spine trauma
- Chest, cardiac, and blood vessel or vascular trauma
- Complex fractures of the pelvis
- Orthopedic trauma

The main difference in how well and how comprehensively a hospital cares for trauma is based not on the emergency department but on surgical and intensive care. In trauma, as you probably have figured out, surgery is the real treatment. Of almost equal importance is the postoperative care or intensive care unit's ability to support the unique challenges of trauma. Additionally, the special capability of the anesthesiology department and the equipment that must support certain types of trauma care (CT scans, cardiopulmonary bypass) are critically important.

Standards for trauma care in the United States are established by the American College of Surgeons (ACS), who also offer special training for physicians (advanced trauma life support). ACS has also created the criteria for hospitals that determine a certain level of capability.

The ACS does not *officially* designate specific hospitals as trauma centers, and numerous US hospitals that are not verified by ACS claim trauma center designation. Most states have passed legislation that determines the process for designation of trauma centers within their state. The ACS describes this responsibility as "a geopolitical process by which empowered entities, government or otherwise, are authorized to designate." The ACS's self-appointed mission is limited to confirming and reporting on any given hospital's ability to comply with the ACS standard of care in its *Resources for Optimal Care of the Injured Patient.*

A hospital can receive trauma center verification by meeting the specific criteria established by the ACS and passing a site review by the Verification Review Committee. Remember though, official designation as a trauma center is determined by individual state law provisions. Not every state utilizes the ACS criteria. In general, trauma centers are classified by "level" designation: Level I is the highest, and Level III the lowest. Some states have five designated levels, in which case Level V is the lowest. There are also special designations for pediatric trauma.

It is extremely important for you to know how states determine the way that trauma classification will be recognized within their borders. Some states mirror the ACS guidelines completely. Others do so partially: for example, Levels I and II meet ACS criteria, but there are different criteria for Levels III and IV. Others create their own criteria entirely.

Generally speaking, Level I classification indicates the most comprehensive ability to address trauma. The difference in Levels I and II is generally *immediate* neurosurgical capability. Many hospitals have neurosurgical support in all its forms. The difference is whether there is an in-house resident and supervisory attending physician or the surgeon has to be called in.

And now for some useful information about trauma. Here are some terms that you may encounter, including a little background on each.

The Golden Hour

This term is actually being reconsidered in some academic settings. It still prevails in prehospital care. It's a concept that a person with certain types of bleeding or injury has a greater chance of survival if treated in a trauma center within an hour. The term hearkens back to the Vietnam War, when combat-injured personnel had greater survival rates after rapid helicopter evacuations because they got to the right place at the right time. In fact, the sooner an individual with "significant trauma" is evaluated and treated, the better, so don't stop at a donut shop on the way to the hospital.

Fingers Spread across the Pelvis

Okay, this isn't as nutty as it sounds. There are certain bone injuries that are often underestimated and that can kill you. These are examples, but they illustrate the potential blood loss for a person after a bone fracture. Your results may vary, so don't mess around.

- A closed femur (thigh bone) fracture, 1.5 liters
- A fractured pelvis, 3 liters
- A fractured rib, 150 milliliters (each rib)
- After injury resulting in hemothorax (Doesn't that sound like a Dr. Seuss character?), on average up to 2 liters can pool in the chest cavity
- Tibial (lower leg) and humeral (upper arm) fractures, open wounds the size of an adult hand, and a clot the size of an adult fist, 0.5 liter each

When you consider that you have a large plexus of veins (remember to spread three fingers over the lower abdomen to illustrate) and the shift of the pelvis can lacerate those, you can better understand that what you don't see might just hurt you. Also consider that a person who weights 70 kilograms contains only 5 liters of blood, so the amount of blood loss can be significant.

Dr. Seuss Failed Characters Hall of Fame
Entry #22   The Hemothorax

Chest Trauma

If you are in a car accident and sustain an injury to the chest, don't take it lightly. You may feel "okay," but you could have some injuries that bleed very slowly and then can cause huge risk to life. For example, in a condition known as tamponade, the bruised heart bleeds into the surrounding sac until the pressure decreases the heart's normal effective pumping. Short message: go to the hospital and get it checked out.

Brain Trauma

My grandmother was a wealth of medical horror stories when I was a kid. Her favorite, which fits right in here, was about some obscure cousin who was in a logging accident and sustained a blow to the head. The way she told it, he popped right up after the injury and was fine—no loss of consciousness, no nausea, no nothing. He went on his merry way, but right in the middle of dinner that night he nosed over dead, "right in the gravy bowl." Now, I don't know about all that, but the scientist in me is also suspicious of the family recipe for gravy. Nevertheless, the story is pretty good for illustrating the delayed lethal effects of a head injury. There are a lot of such tales of sudden mental decompensation and death from an intracranial bleed. You may hear the terms "epidural hematoma" and "subdural hematoma." I am going to way oversimplify, but here is what those terms mean.

Epidural hematoma: This is usually quick. It is more often seen in younger people. It is usually caused by an artery being torn between the dura, a tough membrane between the skull and the brain. It expands pretty fast (hours) and eventually shoves the brain to one side, squeezing it. If not treated, it will kill the patient. Epidural hematomas are classically seen after a person is struck in the head, is knocked out momentarily, and awakens, seemingly fine.

Subdural hematoma: This is usually slow. It is more often seen in older people, meaning over 45 (I don't like that definition of "older" either). It is usually caused by a vein being torn between the dura and an inner membrane called the arachnoid (sounds like a Martian spider). It expands really slowly (even days to a week). It can also kill you with a similar mechanism to the epidural, but often the patient will not be knocked out and will ignore symptoms longer because they are slower to emerge.

In any case, if you suffer a head trauma, go to the hospital and, for crying out loud, don't drive yourself.

BURNS

Anyone who has experienced a burn, especially a severe burn, knows that a burn is a kind of trauma. The unique pathology or effect on the body, however, and the specialized training, equipment, and support services needed to address the unique needs of this type of care make it a unique category. In the United States, it is estimated that there are approximately 1,800 burn beds. The American Burn Association (ABA) establishes the standard for burn center care. Due to the special requirements and the limited number of qualifying centers, most hospitals that provide nonburn trauma care have a formalized or written agreement for referring patients to a burn center. A burn center may treat adults, children, or both. Burn injuries that should be referred to a burn center include the following:

1. Partial-thickness burns of greater than 10 percent of the total body surface area
2. Burns that involve the face, hands, feet, genitalia, perineum, or major joints
3. Third-degree burns in any age group
4. Electrical burns, including lightning injury
5. Chemical burns
6. Inhalation injuries
7. Burn injury in patients with preexisting medical disorders that could complicate management, prolong recovery, or increase mortality
8. Any patients with burns and additional trauma (such as fractures) in which the burn injury poses the greatest risk of death or disability. In such cases, if the trauma poses the greater immediate risk, the patient's condition may be stabilized initially in a trauma center before transfer to a burn center. Physician judgment will be necessary in such situations and should be in concert with the regional medical control plan and triage protocols.

9. Burned children in hospitals without qualified personnel or equipment for the care of children

10. Burn injury in patients who will require special social, emotional, or rehabilitative intervention

STROKE

Stroke care is very complex to describe. While trauma and burn care have established standards, and even though these standards are not uniformly applied across the country, they are still much more uniform than those applied to stroke care. To understand the criteria and classification of "stroke centers or hospitals," you need to understand that the word *stroke* can have different meanings, and the respective treatments make the classification somewhat tricky. As a physician, I often hear people describe a diagnosis of "stroke" without really understanding the underlying pathology or disease process of the brain.

Blockage can be caused by atherosclerotic plaques or the fatty buildup that we often think of as occurring in the coronary arteries of the heart

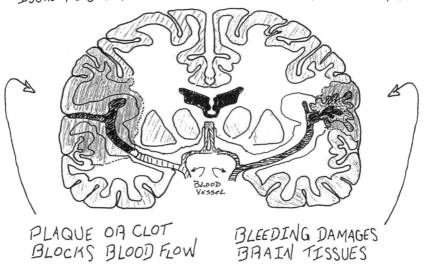

THE HUMAN BRAIN

ISCHEMIC STROKE

HEMORRHAGIC STROKE

BLOOD VESSEL

PLAQUE OR CLOT BLOCKS BLOOD FLOW

BLEEDING DAMAGES BRAIN TISSUES

and leading to a heart attack. That is logical, as the mechanism is the same. The blood flow is blocked off, and the "downstream" tissues and cells literally starve for oxygen and blood. If this starvation goes on long enough, the tissue dies (infarction). The same thing can happen in the brain as the result of an ischemic stroke.

Transient ischemic attacks (TIAs) are small blockage or ischemic events that resolve on their own without therapy. They are also distinguished by not causing permanent damage. The problem with misidentifying a stroke as a TIA is that it can delay proper care, with devastating effects. In short, if you are experiencing the symptoms of confusion, slurred speech, visual changes, or other neurological alteration, seek emergency care.

Hemorrhagic strokes are caused by bleeding in the brain. This type of stroke occurs as the result of an aneurysm (ballooning, weakened blood vessel that may rupture) or other vascular (blood vessel) event. The symptoms are the same as those for an ischemic stroke, but the causes and thus the cures are very different. In fact, the treatment for an ischemic stroke involves blood thinning, which would be devastatingly bad if the stroke is caused by bleeding. For this reason the diagnostic evaluation in the hospital is incredibly important, and given the need for quick intervention in order to save as much tissue in the brain as possible, speed in diagnosis is critical.

Be aware of these stroke symptoms:

- Trouble walking
- Trouble speaking or understanding
- New onset of paralysis and/or numbness of the face, arm, or leg
- New onset of trouble seeing
- Headache with or without nausea and vomiting

A quick story about symptoms. One time when I was in medical school, we were on "rounds" (the daily or twice-daily visitation that physicians make on their admitted patients). I was working for a faculty physician who was notorious for being "clever." In my opinion he liked messing with students by asking difficult questions. As it stood, we were in a cluster of interns, residents, and students, and he was asking a classmate of mine for a differential diagnosis on a patient who had presented to the hospital in a confused state. The man had been acutely exhibiting some inappropriate behavior. He had been making uncharacteristic lascivious advances on his ninety-year-old neighbor, appeared disoriented, showed poor concentration, and complained of nausea and a loss of appetite.

Following his admission to the hospital, he had received an IV and fluids and showed significant improvement. My classmate did a good job, describing the history and course of the patient and listed among possible causes for his initial symptoms a cerebrovascular event or stroke and/or dehydration.

The faculty physician, or "attending," then went around the group asking for additional possibilities. Now, this was a big group, and the major reasonable possibilities were being offered.

"Drug or chemical toxicity," said a resident.

"Okay," said the attending.

"Infection," added another.

"Metabolic causes," said an intern.

"Mmmm-hmmm," said the attending.

And so on it went. Pretty soon all the "good diseases" were taken, and still the attending was asking if anyone had any other offerings. He went one by one, dismissing some of the more desperate guesses. He finally arrived at me.

"What do you think it could be that hasn't already been said? Inappropriate behavior, confusion, poor concentration, and nausea . . . anything else it could be?"

"Well," I said, "I suppose it could be love."

He didn't react, but from then on, he started calling on me earlier in the process.

The Joint Commission (formerly known as the Joint Commission for the Accreditation of Healthcare Organizations, JACHO), or the TJC, has created standards for accreditation to provide some guidance in language and establish criteria for all stroke care.

The criteria designate two types of stroke centers: primary and comprehensive. This language really means something for you as a patient. The main difference is that primary stroke centers are equipped (CT and MRI scanners) and able (properly trained and quickly available neurologists) to diagnose within a short period of time and treat ischemic strokes (with

Joint Commission

Founded in 1951, The Joint Commission seeks to continuously improve health care for the public, in collaboration with other stakeholders, by evaluating healthcare organizations and inspiring them to excel in providing safe and effective care of the highest quality and value. The Joint Commission evaluates and accredits more than 19,000 healthcare organizations and programs in the United States. An independent, not-for-profit organization, The Joint Commission is the nation's oldest and largest standards-setting and accrediting body in health care. To earn and maintain The Joint Commission's Gold Seal of Approval™, an organization must undergo an on-site survey by a Joint Commission survey team at least every three years. (Laboratories must be surveyed every two years.)

Our Mission: To continuously improve health care for the public, in collaboration with other stakeholders, by evaluating healthcare organizations and inspiring them to excel in providing safe and effective care of the highest quality and value.

Vision Statement: All people always experience the safest, highest quality, best-value health care across all settings.
Source: The Joint Commission

drugs) quickly. And they are able to transfer patients with hemorrhagic strokes to a comprehensive stroke center quickly for surgery. Comprehensive stroke centers must be able to do everything a primary stroke center can, but additionally must be able to quickly begin operating on a bleeding source in the brain.

What we are talking about here is capability. Remember that capability means immediate access to qualified surgeons and supporting services like medications, operating rooms, and anesthesiologists. Following is a detailed description of TJC criteria.

Requirements Specific to Primary Stroke Center Certification

a. A CT scan or MRI scanner must be available 24 hours each day, and should be reserved for stroke patients within 25 minutes of being ordered

b. Access to neurosurgical services (access to a brain surgeon)

c. Laboratory tests of patients with acute stroke must be completed within 45 minutes of being ordered

d. A physician with expertise in interpreting CT or MRI studies must be available within 20 minutes of being asked to read a study

e. A written t-PA (clot busting drug) protocol must exist in the emergency department

f. The medical organization must have a declared and established commitment for acute stroke care

g. The hospital must have written acute stroke "clinical pathways" or "care maps"

h. An acute stroke team, including a physician and at least one other healthcare professional, must be available around the clock

i. The hospital must follow long-term stroke treatment outcomes, and design quality improvement activities

j. Emergency staff must have completed formal training in acute stroke treatments

k. The hospital must have a "stroke unit"

l. There must be a designated stroke center director

m. The stroke team must schedule stroke medical education sessions for stroke staff

n. The hospital must provide formal stroke training for ambulance crews

Requirements Specific to Comprehensive Stroke Center Certification

a. The Comprehensive Stroke Center performs advanced imaging with multi-modal imaging capabilities including:

- Carotid duplex ultrasound
- Catheter angiography
- CT angiography available 24 hours a day, 7 days a week
- MRI, including diffusion weighted MRI, available 24 hours a day, 7 days a week
- Extracranial ultrasonography
- MR angiography-MRA available 24 hours a day, 7 days a week
- Transcranial Doppler
- Transesophageal Echocardiography
- Transthoracic Echocardiography

b. The Comprehensive Stroke Center has the capacity to perform microsurgical neurovascular clipping of aneurysms when indicated.

c. The Comprehensive Stroke Center has the capacity to perform neuro-endovascular coiling of aneurysms when indicated.

d. The Comprehensive Stroke Center has the capacity to perform stenting of extracranial carotid arteries when indicated.

e. The Comprehensive Stroke Center has the capacity to perform carotid endarterectomy (CEA) when indicated.

f. The Comprehensive Stroke Center has an intensive care unit (ICU) for complex stroke patients that includes staff and licensed independent practitioners with the expertise and experience to provide neuro-critical care.

g. Protocols for care demonstrate that the Comprehensive Stroke Center:
   - Addresses evidence-based endovascular procedures including exclusion criteria.
   - Addresses the circumstances in which the hospital would not accept patients for neurosurgical and cerebrovascular surgery.

h. Protocols for care demonstrate that the Comprehensive Stroke Center addresses ongoing collaboration with emergency medical staff (EMS) including an annual collaborative review of protocols.

Of the specialty capabilities that hospitals provide, perhaps the most universal is cardiac care. Yet, of the specialties described in this chapter, it is the one whose facility criteria are considered still in progress. At the time of printing, the criteria for Cardiac Centers of Excellence was still being discussed by the American Heart Association with a great deal of the supportive work put forth by the AHA Hospital Accreditation Science Committee.

There are a number of reasons that there is not an "official" uniform standard and provision across the United States. They include cost—this sort of capability does have a cost—politics—whether there are competing entities nearby—the effort made to meet the described requirements, and estimated need in a community or area. There are plenty of other good books on this issue, but suffice it to say that you will want to make sure you ask your local hospitals about the kinds of cardiac care they can provide before you need to use them.

With this qualification stated, it must be said that the AHA is one of the most effective organizations for supporting research, standards, and education and fostering grassroots and professional awareness and heart and—with its associated organization the American Stroke Association—stroke care.

The AHA is the organizational body that evaluates and determines the recommendations for and establishment of guidelines for cardiopulmonary resuscitation. It also does the same for the type of adult and pediatric cardiac care provided by advanced-level providers such as paramedics. These two programs are known as Advanced Cardiac Life Support (ACLS) and Pediatric Advanced Life Support (PALS).

In short, it is desirable for hospitals to have these capabilities in order to provide the most comprehensive levels of care:

a. 24/7 cardiac catheterization capability, including rapid access (less than 30 minutes) to radiologists, cardiologists, and surgeons. Cardiac "caths" are done to assess the blockage of coronary vessels and sometimes are used to introduce a treatment like a stent.

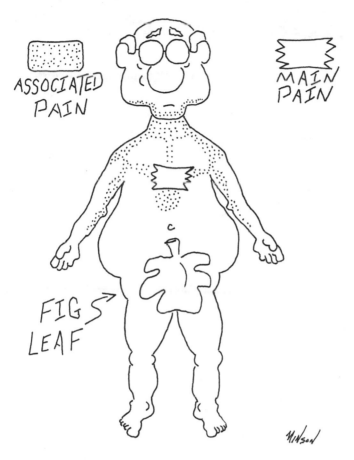

HEART ATTACK PAIN PATTERNS

ASSOCIATED PAIN

MAIN PAIN

FIG LEAF

b. 24/7 laboratory capability to diagnose myocardial infarction (prolonged ischemia that results in permanent cell death) or injury to the heart and to guide definitive treatment

c. Many systems advocate for the ability to go from ER door to catheterization within 90 minutes for select criteria

d. The ability to provide surgical treatment as required within one hour of event onset (this could be for surgery on the heart or the blood vessels of the heart)

e. (Intensive) Cardiac Care Unit capability, with properly trained support doctors and nurses as well as the necessary equipment

The American Heart Association (AHA) is a nonprofit organization in the United States that acts to reduce the risk of stroke and coronary heart disease. The AHA, headquartered in Dallas, Texas, provides funding for medical research, education, and community services. It is a national voluntary health agency whose mission is "Building healthier lives, free of cardiovascular diseases and stroke." Its motto is "Learn and Live." The AHA offers the most widely accepted certification for basic life support (BLS) and is now also a provider of training for first aid, in addition to CPR. The AHA operates an affiliated organization, the American Stroke Association, which focuses on care, research, and prevention of strokes. The AHA publishes CPR guidelines every six years.

WHAT YOU CAN DO

- Visit your local hospitals before you are ill.
- Do your homework (read more than just this book).
- Be courteous and schedule an appointment or tour.
- Galvanize your community (get a group of similarly interested friends) to become informed.
- Ask about the elements described in this chapter and what exactly your hospitals can do and how they are credentialed.
- Ask about trauma level (What standard? What agreements for transfer? How long would transfer be? How many cases have they seen in the last year, and when are they up for renewal of their status?). Are the surgeons and staff in-house or must they be called in for these situations:

- Neuro/brain trauma?
- Orthopedics: Can they fix a broken femur and/or a complicated pelvis fracture?
- Chest trauma including large blood vessel? Can they go on bypass emergently?

- Pediatric?
- Cardiac care? Ask for the statistics. They should have available the number of catheterizations and complication rates per year. Can they do a coronary bypass procedure immediately if something goes wrong during a catheterization? How far and how long if transfer is required?
- Stroke care? Are they TJC accredited as a primary or secondary center? If not, where is the closest?
- Emergency care? Is the emergency department staffed 24/7? This is important in certain rural or frontier areas. What in-house and transfer arrangements do they have?

Scouting the Healthcare Community

The following is a chart you can use to make sure you are asking the right questions when you assess the hospitals in your area. It should be used *before* you have an emergency, not after.

You see how important it is to have properly researched your own local hospitals. I've said it before, but I'll reiterate: the time to do this is before you are sick or injured. One thing you might do is ask your physician where he would go if he had the problems of trauma, stroke, burns, or cardiac issues. If it is what your doctor prefers, you wouldn't want any less. So, put down this book and pick up the phone, and maybe schedule a tour of your local hospitals. Better yet, get with your preferred civic organization or get a group of friends together and request a meeting with a representative from the different hospitals' administration. They may be bowled over by the level of detail you are requesting, but they should respect you.

Just think of it as informed consumerism. Think of it as civic responsibility, or just think of it as self-defense. It may just change where you go and how well you do.

Hospital Survey Tool

Hospital name/ ACS trauma level	Total admission beds/ ED beds/Available beds	ICU/ Types/ Total beds/ Total	Specialty capacities care/Dialysis/Negative pressure rooms/ Total	OR types/ Available

Specialty Considerations: Surgical On-Call/Admitting
(Please circle all that are applicable and comment as desired.)

Orthopedics   Y/N   Pelvis/Spine/Cervical spine _____
_____
_____

ABA classified burns   Y/N _____
_____
_____

Urology   Y/N _____
_____
_____

Vascular   Y/N _____
_____
_____

Cardiothoracic   Y/N   Bypass capability   Y/N _____
_____
_____

(A more expanded version of this sheet is available at www.PrepareToDefendYourself Health.com)

CHAPTER 5

THE ADMISSION

YOU ARE GOING IN!

YOU ARE GOING IN!

S o, you have recovered from your wolverine attack, survived the traumatic entry into the OLPCHS, and made it back home, but now something else has come up. You have seen your primary-care physician or the PA or the ANP and it has been determined something needs "fixing." You are going to require an *elective procedure.* This is catch-all language for nonemergent, non-life-threatening, or limb-saving surgery. Think bunionectomies or breast augmentations. While elective procedure sounds like a less intense situation, when it is about to happen to *you*, it isn't. The downside is that you will have something done. The upside is that you have some time to prepare. So how do you do that? Perhaps a real-life anecdote would help.

Recently, someone I care about, someone I actually love, was faced with needing surgery. Added to that was the possibility that the surgeon would find a malignancy. As you know, I am a physician, yet with the very personal nature of this, I found myself challenged to prepare. The distraction of that potential was such that while I easily remembered the preoperative checklist and issues related to the procedure to come, the peripheral details—those issues that seem minute but that can make the difference between an uneventful course and a nightmare—were not so easily captured. I could recall medication lists and what to relate to the anesthesiologist, the surgeon, and the pre-op nurse. But had I done the shopping for the week after we were home? Did I have the materials necessary to facilitate bedside bathing? Or the transition to the shower or the tub that, I would learn, required advanced feats of engineering, strength, and flexibility? What about communications, which could make the difference in security for a bed-bound individual or panic? Had I anticipated the challenges there? Doesn't sound like a big deal, but guess what? It was. And I hadn't even started considering the unique experience of going to the bathroom during home convalescence!

Of course, the procedure was scheduled at OLPCHS, which went through all kinds of public relations communications but, to my educated estimation, left out the practical things that could make a huge difference in how well we did. The useful things I mentioned earlier were not covered at all.

You're probably wondering why after the experience I detailed in the introduction, I would go back to them. Two words: *insurance carrier.*

Based on our insurance provision, OLPCHS was our best and only real option, unless I wanted to take on a potential $70,000 debt, which might be even higher if the finding was cancer and additional treatment was required.

As chance would have it, almost everything that could go wrong with my loved one's experience in the hospital and immediately afterward did. First we were told to arrive at the hospital at 6 a.m., as she was scheduled for some bleeding studies prior to surgery along with a dose of a critical clotting factor.

When the preoperative staff found out she was not going home at the end of the day but instead was going to be admitted, they decided to attend to other cases classified as "day surgeries," and the lab studies were delayed. Because the labs were delayed and the necessary medication administration was delayed, her case was also delayed.

Here's where it gets interesting, and had we lacked the insight of insiders, we would not have been able to defend ourselves. Because of the delayed lab and the delayed medication and then the delay to my beloved's case starting, and because she had been n.p.o. or "nothing by mouth" since midnight the night before, she was approaching 13 hours without anything to eat or drink. That time frame coincided ironically with lunchtime for the operating room staff. So while they attempted to spell the staff to eat, she waited even longer. Finally she made it into the operating room (OR).

The case was more arduous than expected, and the hours dragged. Somewhere around 7:00 p.m. the surgical waiting-room volunteers went home. Several of us in the waiting area inquired after our family members. We were told "someone" would let us know "something," and we were given a phone number to call at our convenience. The result was confusing and disconcerting. Three hours later and four hours past due— it is amazing the possibilities you entertain—the surgeon emerged and reported that the surgery had been far more difficult than expected and that we had to wait for the final pathology report to determine whether the result was benign.

From that point things really went downhill. In the wee hours, the IV ran dry and my beloved's veins "collapsed," so her antibiotics and pain medication could not be given. In a short time, my beloved began experiencing profound pain and nausea. Since the postoperative orders did not provide for anything other than medication through the IV, the staff could not help. Things went from bad to worse as she was now approaching twenty-four hours without adequate hydration, and she was becoming dangerously dehydrated. Several failed attempts by the staff at starting another IV led to even fewer options, as the veins were now traumatized and could not be used. Fortunately, I was able to be there and advocated that a central line be inserted (an IV placed in a large interior vein, like the jugular), but there was a backlog of patients waiting for a similar procedure. The conversation became quite strident to the point of a complaint about the critical nature of the inattention and slow resolution going to the hospital's administration. Amazingly, the apologies piled up, but no action followed. The situation was approaching a dangerously critical point since no blood tests had been feasible, so additional clotting factor was not administered, the dehydration worsened, the nausea and vomiting continued, and the antibiotics and pain medication went ungiven.

And all the while, we still did not know if we were dealing with cancer . . .

I am glad that I was there. I am glad I have the training and an insider's awareness of what to do to and how to apply pressure to get it done. Even so, the *system* proved a formidable opponent. So, with all of that as justification, I'd like to offer the following so you can approach and hopefully navigate your own hospital stay with greater safety and self-empowerment.

Communication

In a world where we are so much more technologically and socially connected than ever before, where we can take and send a picture or a thought with almost regrettably immediate ability, it's ironic that we seem to still have as many or more interpersonal communication failures. Communication failure is arguably one of the biggest factors in problems occurring for patients. It ranges from insurance authorizations, to dialogue between primary-care physicians and "in-house" providers, to medication errors. It is also where you as a patient can do the most to protect yourself. That means preparation.

WHAT YOU CAN DO

- Make copies of your ID and secure your originals in a safe place at home for backup.
- Create and assign a power of access or attorney to someone or an advanced directive, if that is appropriate.
- In chapter 3 I recommended that you create a medical form and have it appropriately available for EMS. Make sure to take that to the hospital with you. Better yet, copy it. Scan it.
- Have multiple modes to keep your records: flash drive, disc, a hard copy (on paper), and so on.
- Your medical information is yours. Not the doctor's. Not the hospital's. Make sure you obtain and maintain copies of your medical records. Entrust a copy of them to a trusted advocate, friend, or relative.
- Make a small hospital survival pack that has your pertinent information. Maybe use an organizer to categorize information (labs, X-rays, etc.). Include home stuff, business stuff, personal stuff, a to-do list while still in the hospital.
- Include insurance cards, hard copies of e-mails that authorized approvals by the insurance provider. (Get names, dates, and guaranteeing language.) At the admission or entry desk is not where you want to be negotiating the terms of approvals and authorization.

Something Legal

Earlier I used the terms "power of attorney" and "advanced directive." I want to elaborate on what that means and how you establish either one. I am no attorney, so if this piques your interest, you should explore it further online and then with your legal adviser. Many state attorney's offices have boilerplate language that you can tailor to your situation. This is often available online.

"Power of attorney" is a term for your authorization of another trusted individual to speak for you and make official decisions for you in the event that you cannot. The person you name is called the *attorney in fact* or *agent*. Despite the title, the person you designate does not have to be a lawyer. The person who signs a power of attorney making someone else his or her agent is called the *principal*. That's you. A power of attorney may be for a limited purpose and a limited time period, or it can be general and have no expiration date.

The two types of powers of attorney that people use the most are "general" and "special." A special power of attorney gives the agent the right to do a certain thing within a certain period of time, for example, sign the papers needed to transfer property. This limits the right of the person you selected to act for you. A general power of attorney gives the agent the right to do many things. The individual can transfer title to your car or property, open or close bank accounts, transfer certificates of deposit, and provide money for your family. This kind of power of attorney gives the agent a lot of responsibility, so the agent should be someone who is trustworthy and honest. There is a difference between a *general* and a *special* power of attorney. If you become unable to handle your affairs (incompetent), a special power of attorney may end. If you have signed a durable power of attorney, the agent still has the power to handle your affairs if you become incompetent.

For the purposes of this book, we will focus on the medical power of attorney, which is a type of durable power of attorney. This type of power has certain limitations. Your agent can make medical decisions for you only when you cannot make decisions for yourself. For this to apply, your doctor must affirm, in writing, that you cannot make your own healthcare decisions. The doctor's certification then goes in your medical file.

Your agent can make medical decisions for you only until you are able to make them again. You can also revoke or cancel your medical power of attorney at any time. In short, the agent can make healthcare decisions for you with some limitations. This includes healthcare decisions that agree or don't agree to medical procedures or services to diagnose or treat your physical or mental condition. Your agent has to talk to your doctors before making medical decisions. Your agent can also see your medical and hospital records. Your agent cannot agree to hospitalize you for mental health treatment, agree to convulsive treatment or psychosurgery, agree to an abortion, or refuse care that will keep you comfortable.

Advanced directives are written specifications about what kinds of treatments you do and don't want. They are most commonly known for accompanying patients with a terminal illness, but they can be used by anyone for any kind of medical contingency. Think about a young healthy person who wants only certain things done in case he or she has an accident and never regains consciousness. This can also include elements of organ donation and dedication of your remains for medical studies or training physicians at medical schools. These sorts of conditional documents often go along with a power of attorney, but you can have an advanced directive even without an attorney in fact or agent. Regardless of whether you go all out and provide these legal contingencies, make sure you consult a *real* attorney and the laws of your state.

The Advocate

Have an advocate. There is safety in numbers, and we are after all herd animals. In this case, we benefit from acting like it. The advocate is not necessarily someone with power of attorney. In fact, this is just someone you trust, who has your interests at heart. Hopefully, this person is also informed and smart. You will probably not be up to fighting your own battles before or after surgery, so you need this. Rich people have advocates (guns for hire). You should too. Think about it like this: in scuba diving, rock climbing, or lion taming, experts advocate the buddy system. This is no less necessary regarding hospitalization.

Day Surgery Perils vs. Postoperative Admission

Most physicians and many surgical centers schedule day surgery cases and postoperative admission cases for the same day. This is a little insider information, a little inside baseball as my grandmother used to say, that will serve you well. Because day surgery is hopefully just that, a surgery followed by discharge to home, it is usually scheduled earlier to give the patient the most time to recover before being sent out of the hospital where there is not the same post-op support as for those admitted *to* the hospital. Generally, day surgery cases are the first cases of the day.

Why do you care? Well, would you rather have a surgical team awake, alert, and energized, or at the end of the day when they have been operating for a stretch? Operating room personnel get tired and hungry just like everybody else. They think about their kids and the end of the school day and what to make for dinner. It's very human, yet what can you do about it? It all goes back to communication and being informed. Ask your primary-care physician to advise you. Ask questions of your surgeon. What time will my surgery start? Not when does the surgery at the hospital start, but when will *my* surgery start? This matters especially if you have a condition that can be complicated by not being able to ingest anything, such as diabetics or certain people with hypertension.

You are going to want to have certain conversations for certain members of your care team. Sometimes the conversation will be the same for different members of the team. You'll have questions for each, and you should have them organized before you encounter these folks. What follows is a legend of the different key specialists and what questions go with each. Conversations can also be broken down by specialty and categorized by chronology:

- Questions for the anesthesiologist (A)
- Questions for the surgeon (S)
- Questions for the hospitalist (H)
- Questions for your primary-care physician or provider (PCP)
- Questions for your medical specialist (MS)
- Questions at your pre-op evaluation (S, PCP, MS, maybe A)
- Questions immediately before surgery (at the hospital) (S, A)
- Questions after surgery (H, PCP, MS, S)
- Questions for when you are discharged (PCP, S)

Let's expand on that chronology a bit. When you meet with your surgeon, at his or her office, well before you even enter the hospital, go into the discussion having done your homework. Read, read, read everything you can, online and off. The Internet is a great tool, not because it will tell you what you need to know—though it can somewhat—but because it can steer you to other reference materials. Some are listed at the end of this book. As I said earlier, there are questions you will want to pose to each member of the team. Here are a few things you should look into and consider asking your surgeon (S) about:

- What is the success rate of the procedure planned? What is that particular surgeon's experience with success, percentage-wise? Ask for the numbers! Ask how many of these procedures he or she has done. (S)
- What are the benefits of this procedure? What is the success rate in general and in that surgeon's personal experience? Don't be scared of offending anyone. This should be a frank conversation. These people are going to be doing all kinds of things for and to you. You've a right to know. (S, PCP, MS)
- What are my other therapeutic options? How do they compare in the above categories? What could happen if I decide not to have the procedure? (S, PCP, MS)
- Where will the surgery be conducted? What is the infection and complication rate of that facility? Will it be a day surgery, or will I be admitted? Consider touring the facility in advance whenever you have time. Again, would you buy anything else without some consumer evaluation? I would guess not. Then why would you let them anesthetize, cut, and treat you without the same scrutiny? Ask your PCP for an evaluation of the hospital for your type of procedure. Ask your PCP if he or she would go there for the same problem. (S, PCP, MS)
- When am I going to be on the surgery schedule? In general, the calendar does matter. This will probably be a controversial point, but in my experience it is best to be the first case of the day. The surgeon will be fresh, caffeinated, and nourished, and the staff will also be fresh. Having them all less fatigued will diminish the potential of the issues of switching out staff in the OR. You definitely want to assure this! (S)
- Can I continue to take my prescribed medication before the procedure? This may also involve a conversation with your primary-care doctor and the specialist. *Do not be afraid to ask for a conference call* to include your primary or specialist, the surgeon, and you. Take the lead and suggest this. Alteration of medications preoperatively must be spelled out and communicated in hard copy, meaning you need to have it written

down and signed off by the physician(s). Ask for and maintain a copy. (S, PCP, MS)

- Is there any medication I should not take? Take it one step beyond medication. Add to this list whether you should continue your dietary supplements, herbal self-treatments, and the like. It is surprising how much of an impact they may have. (S, PCP, MS)
- What medications will I need immediately postoperatively? In the hospital? At home? Request that the surgeon write your post-op prescriptions and give them to you well before you are scheduled for surgery. Why? Because medications, like anything else, may be in short supply. The last thing you want to experience, as you are in pain and unsteady, is the additional stress of discovering that a pharmacy is out of stock, or that you have to now travel somewhere else for a medication while you are in a compromised state. This also applies to special braces, wound-care supplies, and more, not just medications. (S, A, MS, PCP)
- Request a conversation with the anesthesiologist. When you do, be sure to ask what type of anesthetic you will receive. Be prepared to ask whether this will be a *general*, a *regional*, or a *local* anesthetic. Don't just be placated with, "You are going to go to sleep now." It's inaccurate, and it's not respectful to you. (S, A)

Anesthesia Terms You Should Know

Various types of anesthesia may be used during your procedure.

GENERAL ANESTHESIA

General anesthesia (GA) is the state produced when a patient receives medications for amnesia, analgesia (pain blocking), muscle paralysis (sometimes), and sedation (decreased cognition). An anesthetized patient can be thought of as being in a controlled, reversible state of unconsciousness. Anesthesia enables a patient to tolerate surgical procedures that

ANESTHESIOLOGIST EMPATHY

would otherwise inflict unbearable pain, potentiate extreme physiologic reactions like increases in blood pressure, and result in unpleasant or traumatic memories.

The combination of anesthetic agents used for general anesthesia often leaves a patient with the following collection of clinical signs and symptoms:

1. Unarousable even by painful stimuli
2. Unable to remember what happened (amnesia)
3. Potentially unable to maintain adequate upper airway (mouth and throat) protection and/or breathe adequately as a result of muscle paralysis
4. Cardiovascular changes secondary to stimulant/depressant effects of anesthetic agents

This state can be thought of as a controlled, induced coma. The physical dynamics of breathing may be reversed. Normally we use negative pressure to "draw" a breath. The diaphragm contracts to pull air in. A ventilator uses "positive pressure" or pumps air in. This is important, as it can negatively affect the cardiovascular system and the lungs of some patients.

When you have a regional anesthetic, your anesthesiologist injects medication near a cluster of nerves to numb only the area of your body that requires surgery. Regional anesthesia can include spinal blocks, epidural blocks, or peripheral (arm, leg, or other nerve) blocks. You may remain awake, or you may be given a sedative depending on your anesthesiologist's and your decision. Spinal and epidural blocks involve interrupting sensation from the pelvis, legs, or abdomen by injecting local anesthetic medication in or near the spinal canal. Other blocks can be performed for surgery on your extremities, or limbs, in order to block painful sensations from the arm or leg.

This blockade of sensation can also affect motor control or strength of a limb or region of the body. It can also, depending on the procedure and type of "regional," be used postoperatively for pain management and control. This can be very important. The sharper you are mentally after a surgery, the better you can protect yourself. Ask your anesthesiologist and surgeon about this. It is much more forgiving on the lungs and cardiovascular system. Regardless of whether you are awake for the procedure or truly sedated, you are still breathing on your own but unaware of the surgical activity.

SEDATION

"Sedation" is a misused term and actually involves using sedation medications such as benzodiazepines (like diazepam, also called Valium) and opiates (like morphine) so that you are relaxed and pain-free but still breathing on your own. You may also be somewhat awake, depending on how much medicine you receive. You can understand and answer questions and will be able to follow your physician's instructions. When receiving sedation, you will feel drowsy and may even sleep through much of the procedure but will be easily awakened when spoken to. You may or may not remember being in the operating room. Depending on the "depth," you may sleep through the procedure with little or no memory of it. So, you are kind of "with it" mentally but nowhere near ready to take the SAT.

While you receive sedation during surgery, your vital signs, including heart rate, blood pressure, and oxygen level, will be watched closely in order to avoid sudden changes or complications. You may also receive supplemental oxygen during the surgery, because the sedation decreases your respiratory drive (central nervous system triggers that make you take a breath).

MONITORED ANESTHESIA CARE (MAC)

MAC combines intravenous sedation with local anesthetic infiltration and/or nerve blocks. This is similar to sedation but occurs in an operating room. Procedures such as otoplasty (ear surgery), face-lift, blepharoplasty, or liposuction are examples of surgeries routinely performed under MAC. Patients given monitored anesthesia rather than general anesthesia are (generally) less likely to experience nausea and vomiting and typically can be discharged home more safely and quickly.

LOCAL ANESTHESIA

Local anesthesia can be confused with the description of "local" or even of a regional block, and the sedation can be described as mild, moderate, or deep. "Deep" can actually approach the quality of a general anesthetic. Generally—and this is very general—if it involves a small area or smaller section of a single nerve, then it is a local anesthetic. Think about being "numbed" for suturing of a simple laceration. Local anesthesia encompasses infiltration of the operative site and limited nerve blocks. A nerve block can be labeled minor if one nerve is affected or major if more than one nerve or conduction in a nerve plexus is impeded.

Now we have some background. We can continue with our questions for the anesthesiologist.

- What are the advantages and disadvantages of the type of anesthesia I will receive? (S, A)
- Will I have nausea when I wake up? What will be done for that? (A, S)
- Who will be my anesthesia provider? Will it be a physician or a nurse? (S, A)

- What are the risks associated with this type of anesthesia? (A)
- Will I wake up during the surgery? How will you be sure I don't? (A)
- Are there any specific complications associated with anesthesia and this procedure that I should be aware of? (S, A)
- How long will the entire surgery take? (S, A)
- Are there any permanent or short-term risks to mental function with the chosen anesthesia? (A)
- When will I wake up? (A)
- Will I be in pain when I wake up from the procedure? How will that be addressed? Shots, pills, IV, patient-controlled analgesia (PCA) pump? (S, A)
- After the surgery, can I be placed in a recovery room with a window? (It helps with staying oriented and biologically in sync with the world.) (S)
- When will I be discharged from the hospital? What will be the criteria? Will it just be some percentages-based insurance algorithm? (S, PCP)
- What drugs should I avoid taking in the postoperative period? (S, A)
- How long should I wait before standing or bearing weight after my procedure? (S, PCP, MS)
- Will I need someone to drive me home? Generally the answer to this is yes. Pass the keys over! (S, MS)
- What should I do if I don't feel well after I'm discharged? Whom should I call? (S, PCP, MS)
- When will I be completely healed? (S)
- Are any follow-up appointments necessary? (S, PCP, MS)
- What do I need to do before the procedure? This is a big question, and there are some additional recommendations to follow. This is explained more fully in the section about recovering at home and lifestyle adjustments. (PCP, S)

Doubling Up on Procedures

It's fairly surprising how many people consider having multiple surgeries done simultaneously. "As long as I'm in there" being the thinking. While it's not set in stone that doubling up on procedures is a bad idea, it is not the same thing as having your windshield wipers replaced as long as the car is in the shop for its brakes. Unfortunately, there are some terrible anecdotes from patients about the negative synergy of temporarily disabling procedures.

For example, let's consider that you are having surgery on your bladder. At the same time the surgeon suggests that we could get that pesky bunion fixed as long as we are in there. You are already going to be "asleep," right? The insurance company loves the idea, because you won't incur another cost for a subsequent anesthetic procedure and/or hospitalization. And guess what, you don't even have to stay overnight. You can head home that evening. Everybody wins. Right? Maybe.

Fast-forward and you have been discharged from the day surgery. Depending on the day of the week, holiday schedules, and the like, you will probably be subject to variable levels of post-op support once you are removed from the system.

Recently, there has been a heightened emphasis on phone support for patients, and while this sounds good, it is general support, and generally you will not speak with anyone who was with you during the surgery, during the post-op recovery, or at your discharge.

I'm not advising that you should not have multiple procedures. I'm advising that it should be a carefully considered decision with informed opinions advising you. You—as a patient—should be a well-informed and critical consumer. You should also consider that you will not feel in the post-op period as well as you did pre-op.

Getting Your House in Order

Never have those words mattered more, and frankly, when it comes to your postoperative phase at home, little oversights can become big problems. Most people don't think about the domestic obstacle course that is their home when they are whole. They discover the issues concerning clutter and trip hazards only after they are limited by soreness, splinting, sedation, and the like. This can be a rude and dangerous discovery. While this may seem mundane, I assure you my experience with postoperative declarations of, "I wish I had thought to put steps next to the bed, get that shower chair, get that walker to aid in the seemingly simple act of maneuvering to the bathroom, fill the fridge or . . . kenneled my pet wolverine, before I went in for my surgery" is considerable. This goes back to the subject of having multiple procedures or surgeries and asking realistic questions of your physician. Don't overestimate yourself, or as Clint Eastwood famously said, "Know your limitations."

Consider the double surgeries of bladder reconstruction and bunionectomy mentioned earlier, for example. Think about the loss of balance and the decreased stability of your leg after you get home from the hospital. Remember that your bladder surgeon was clear in advising that you should go to the bathroom the second you feel the urge, and your foot surgeon's warning not to bear weight on your foot wound. Now imagine the ludicrous, undignified, and complex ballet of hobbling to the water closet when nature calls. Want to add to the hilarity? Imagine that your wolverine, Ramon, sees you hopping and takes that as an indication you want to play. Or imagine encountering your great-grandmother's cast-iron rocking chair ("only twelve were known to exist") blocking your path and you get my point.

That might be just a little challenging, yes? If you are into drama, or even comedy, well, good. You are in for a real treat. But in seriousness, the limitations of one post-op restriction may compromise another. Think about that, and you should be realistic and satisfied that you will not have post-op issues that compromise each other when you are finally on your own.

WHAT YOU CAN DO

- As a general rule *underestimate* your post-op self. Consider the embarrassing stuff that most people do not address. Will I have problems with pooping, peeing, brushing my teeth, and cleaning myself? Are there medical devices to help me? Will my eyesight be adequate? Do I need additional magnification? Are there going to be flexibility and strength requirements? Do I need extension arms, a walker, crutches, or something else?

- Just remember that in home health care, pride goeth before a fall, and busted stitches, and a cracked hip! Use the Web, and talk openly with your physician and others who have had similar surgeries. This is where the Internet can be extremely valuable. Check out the blogs. You can ask questions, even delicate ones, anonymously and receive some helpful hints.

- Assess your home. Do you have open and wide avenues for moving to the bathroom, the television, the sink, the refrigerator? If need be, rearrange the furniture. Move that cast-iron rocker. Put steps next to the bed to provide assistance getting in and out. Maybe consider ramps, skyhooks, and so on. Again, do this before the surgery!

- The routine stuff is easily overlooked and still incredibly important. Household management is something better minimized by acting before you are post-op. Pay your bills before you go into the hospital. Arrange for daily activities, like housekeeping and meal preparation, in advance. Clean your house beforehand. Do your grocery shopping, and don't plan on doing any complicated culinary activities immediately after your surgery. You can watch the Food Network but probably should not attempt anything too elaborate. Do laundry, so that is not an issue. Doing this will minimize disruptions and irritations when you are in need of rest and calm.

- Place the telephones close by, and make sure they are fully charged. Have a flashlight at the bedside. Make sure there are fresh batteries in the remotes, smoke detectors, and the like.

- Your concentration and normally razor-sharp mental powers may be affected, so give yourself a break. Make cheat sheets with contact numbers and place them next to the bed. Put a notepad next to the bed or, better, an audio recorder. This way ideas or questions for your health provider and caregivers will not slip your mind.

- Beauty is truth and truth is beauty. That is all ye know and all ye need know. Well, with respect to John Keats, that may not be entirely true, but as a species we care a lot about how we look and how we feel about how we look. Schedule haircuts, manicures, and pedicures, and all the other "cures" that matter before surgery. It is surprising how much that can actually affect a person's overall attitude after an ordeal.

- A word about smoking . . . Seriously? Don't. If you can, quit well before your surgery. If you can't quit, talk honestly about this with your surgeon and the anesthesiologist. Have a plan.

Now you are ready to go to the hospital.

What to Pack?

Consider the following suggestions, but make sure you have cleared these items with your healthcare provider and surgeon.

- Medications. Bring everything you take—including any over-the-counter meds, vitamins, and supplements taken regularly. The medical staff needs to know exactly what each patient is taking, although they often take away the patient's own supply and administer medications on the hospital's schedule.
- Favorite snacks, including juices and other drinks. Just make sure it's nothing requiring refrigeration.
- Fun, not-too-challenging books, magazines, and games. As mentioned earlier, it can be hard to concentrate on anything too intellectual—especially in the first day or two after surgery. So do the *New York Times* crossword puzzle in pencil for a while, or even better, read *People* magazine.
- A DVD player and movies you like.
- A few pictures of important people and favorite things, such as spouse, friends, kids, and pets. Surround yourself with reminders of what really matters!
- A hat, scarf, or other head covering. Many people want to hide their hair when they've been in the hospital for several days

without a shower. This is the real reason why pirates wear kerchiefs on their heads, you know.

- One or two changes of comfortable, loose clothing, including *very loose* pants or shorts, skirts, or dresses . . . or if you are Scottish, kilts . . . that can go over a large bandage, and several changes of underwear and socks. It's not likely that more than one or two outfits will be needed. Clothing is one thing most surgical patients pack far too much of for their first hospital stay.
- An extra blanket, roomy cardigan sweater, or bathrobe for those who get cold easily.
- Cosmetics and toiletries.
- Sleep masks, ear plugs, and/or a white-noise machine.
- Glasses and hearing aids if you need them.

Pre-op and Post-op

Be mindful of hygiene. I'll talk more about this later, but become proficient in the use of the phrase, "Wash those hands, Buster." Don't feel bashful about calling the staff on hygiene and hand washing. They should *all* wash their hands before touching you and again afterward. The *staff* should not be the reason you wind up with a *staph* infection! Get it?

When you leave the operating room, there are only two places you can go. The most likely is the post-anesthesia care unit (PACU), formerly known as the "recovery room." The other, less frequent immediate post-surgical destination is the intensive care unit (ICU).

In the PACU you'll be monitored by a combination of staff while you fully recover your awareness. They will follow the effects of anesthesia and of your surgery. Should something indicating that you need further surgical correction emerge, like bleeding, you might go back to the OR. More than likely though, you will—after clinical improvement landmarks are met—be sent to either the ICU or the "floor" in a low-acuity or low-severity (meaning less carefully monitored) bed on the ward. If you are a day surgery patient, you will go to the day surgery unit, where you will be prepared for discharge to your home.

If you have watched TV, you have seen the intensity of the ICU. It's even in the name. It is a specially equipped and staffed area for patients who need a place that can provide extended monitoring and support. Some of the conditions that require ICU support include aid with ventilation, administration of infusions to support blood pressure and cardiovascular function, and a need for invasive (internal) monitoring for the critical or unstable patient.

THE FLOOR BED OR THE WARD BED

This is the typical post-op or hospital bed. The room may be private or double occupancy or even, as in the old days of medicine, a long row of communal beds separated by curtains. This is for patients who are pretty stable and do not require moment-by-moment scrutiny for their protection. It is where we will focus our discussion on your hospital stay.

Life on the ward could be a book in and of itself, but I think you are better served by receiving some brief survival tips and being alerted to issues that commonly plague patients on the ward. They are in no particular order.

Rest

The most common instruction given, and the most universal expectation by placing a patient in a bed, is that the patient should get *rest*. If you have been in a hospital lately, you realize that rest may very well be one of the most unobtainable commodities around. In fact, it may be nearly impossible. Between the alarms on monitors and machines placed there for your safety, and the comings and goings of staff to administer medications, stick you for blood, or check your vital signs, your room can seem like Grand Central Station. Somewhere in the mix, the most basic fundamental of recovery from a procedure has been sacrificed to all the taskings for the ward staff. Still you have to have rest, so what can you do?

WHAT YOU CAN DO

- Request the bed nearest the window if you will be in a multibed room.
- The hallway is where the noise is. It is where tray carts and med carts crash, where discussions—often emotional ones occur, with people complaining at the nurse's station—happen, and it often carries into the room and keeps patients awake.
- Get a white-noise machine. This can be a godsend, as it creates a cocoon of interference for all those hospital intrusions.
- Use ear plugs, but make sure they do not drown out the important stuff like fire alarms, and that they mold to your ears so as not to injure the canal. They can be a sanity saver if the person in the next bed is moaning or snores.
- Ask your physician to write "do not disturb between x and y hours" to assure you are left to sleep. This is one of the greatest oversights by care providers regarding rest. Left to chance, you are sure to be interrupted by staff, who fit you into their medication, lab, and work schedules. Your rest, and even the consideration of it, is often a secondary consideration.
- Ask the staff to try to coordinate activities like medication administration and blood draws at the same time. Otherwise, you'll be up all night. Again, your physician is key here. Make sure the physician writes an *order* on your *chart*.
- Sleep medications. This is tricky. Many people do not like the idea of a sleeping pill. Personally, I don't either, but there are times when this may be necessary.
- Two things to keep in mind are using drugs to sleep should only be a temporary "fix," and they should not be taken if you cannot be *guaranteed* an uninterrupted sleep cycle. Interruption of sleep periods (less than eight hours) can cause serious problems and lead to certain behaviors that may be mistaken for other issues. So make sure you will get eight uninterrupted hours. Talk with your physician.

Hygiene

If the first casualty of hospitalization is rest, then a close second is hygiene. This is really ironic, given the hospital obsession with and perception of cleanliness. It's true, though. When I mention hygiene, I am talking about two categories of cleanliness: that maintained by the hospital and its staff, and your personal hygiene. Both are important, and while you normally have control of the cleanliness of both yourself and your home environment, hospitalization changes everything.

In the previous chapters I wrote about the appropriateness of visiting, touring, critically shopping, and reviewing your local healthcare options. I mentioned requesting statistics on infections and medical errors. Having that information before you ever enter a hospital is vital. So, let's assume that you have done that before your surgery. Now that you are in and post-op, what should you do? Take control of your hygiene!

Nobody wants to be rude, and when you are somewhat dependent on these people you don't know bringing you food, water, medicine, and other necessities, it may not seem wise to call out their failure to wash their hands or see to the upkeep of your surroundings. It may, however, literally be a matter of your well-being. So speak up. If the nurses, physicians, or any other people enter with the intent of interaction and do not immediately wash their hands *before* they approach you, ask them to. Hospital-based infections can be the most aggressive and devastating you'll encounter, so please don't be ashamed to defend yourself. You have a right, and they have an obligation.

We've talked about *them,* but what about *you* staying clean? What actions can you take? What should you expect?

When was the last time you had a sponge bath? Was it refreshing, fulfilling, satisfactory, and ablutionary? I bet not. In most cases, the desire to keep clean is balanced against the protection of a wound from potential negative effects of water. They do not, however, have to constitute a choice of either/or. In general, and this is *very* general, you have to have a good 24 hours without water on the wound. Rinse-off can occur at 48 hours. You can shower at 48+, then soak at two weeks plus. But ask about this!

There are some dry cleansers and waterless shampoos, but many patients find them less satisfying and not a strong promotion of the sort of appearance they want before the world.

WHAT YOU CAN DO

- Get that haircut or style before going in.
- Make sure you take your favorite toiletries to the hospital with you.
- If there are waterless shampoos or cleansers planned, get some beforehand and see how well they work. Then you know what to expect.
- Ask about beautician services in the hospital. Some have them.
- Remember that "pirate" head covering. You'll see why after a couple of days. It's fashionable and functional, and if you have to board a hostile ship . . .
- Have an advocate if you can. It's amazing what someone brushing or doing your hair can mean.

Delirium, or, I'm Not Crazy; They Just Dress Me This Way!

This is an especially interesting issue, especially for people in the ICU, having a prolonged hospital stay, or the elderly and medicated. Orientation refers to the ability to discern time, place, and sense of self. It is amazing how easily it is compromised. It is also amazing how the hospital experience can contribute to it. If you think about the other issues described—sleep deprivation, medication, pain, an alien environment, and the least flattering wardrobe imaginable—is it any wonder you can become confused and disoriented? This is why having such items of familiarity along with a clock and an electronic calendar or a laptop computer are invaluable. It may also be of value to request that your physician conduct a cognitive exam during your preoperative interview. This will serve as a baseline for your physician to evaluate your mental function after surgery.

Post-op at Home

Now this is all about *logistics*: mobility, support, communication, nourishment, and hygiene. Just as in the hospital, only more so at home, you are on your own.

I have mentioned advocacy many times in this book, but one area where skilled advocacy can make the difference between a smooth course or medical complications is at home. Discuss having a home health visit from a medical provider with your physician before you leave the hospital. If you feel you will need assistance, ask the physician to write an order, and insurance will generally cover it. Don't expect family members to be able to change dressings or evaluate surgical drains or even evaluate your wound. If something goes wrong, they may not have the same objectivity, training, and experience to address it, and you don't want to saddle them with the guilt of a bad outcome. Additionally—and this is no small consideration—by keeping the post-op care in the hands of a professional, you will be less likely to be blamed if something goes wrong.

WOUND CARE

This applies in the hospital as well, but you should be very vigilant about any changes in the level of pain. Healthcare providers ask about pain according to a scale of 1 to 10, with 10 being the worst imaginable. Communicate it like that, and they will act accordingly.

Redness. The fancy term for this is erythema. It's from the Greek *erythros*, meaning "red." It refers to the reaction of tissues and inflammation. It can also be a sign of early infection.

Swelling. This is another sign of abnormality. It can indicate bleeding or poor drainage.

Local heat. This is another indicator of inflammation and possibly infection.

Discharge. Generally, if anything is coming out of a wound other than what your surgeon has anticipated, it's a very bad sign that warrants reporting. If it has color, that should be noted when it is reported. Take pictures of your wound or incision periodically to create a little electronic record. This is often invaluable, as it can be sent to the physician and communicates what is going on without forcing you to travel. It also creates a means for comparison.

FEVER

Fever is pretty nonspecific, but in a postoperative environment there are some general rules that are of value. Fever according to the time line after surgery follows an old mnemonic: Wind, Water, Walking/Veins/Weins, Wound, and Wonder Drugs.

- Wind, postoperative day (POD) 1–2: Think the lungs. Think pneumonia, aspiration, pulmonary embolism.
- Water, POD 3–5: Think urinary tract infection.
- Walking or Weins (pretend you are German), POD 4–6: Think deep venous thrombosis (DVT) progressing to thrombophle-

bitis and embolic events. This is about immobility, so *move*, soldier. Other things that increase the likelihood of DVT include oral contraceptives/hormone replacement therapy, obesity, a central venous catheter, phlebitis, hypercoagulation, pregnancy, malignancy, advanced age, sepsis, and . . . surgery.
- Wound, POD 5–7: Think surgical site, deep and superficial infection.
- Wonder drugs, POD 7+: Think medication effects, IV lines, or reaction to blood products (though this can vary).

DRAINS

Drains are just what you would imagine they are. They are tubes that allow fluid or material to drain out of a surgical incision. Sometimes a drain is inserted so that pressure does not build up inside a wound. This is done for a number of reasons, and the maintenance and care of a drain and the tubing around the wound site are fairly skilled stuff. In general, the big concerns with a drain are blockage and infection.

Blockage occurs because of clots or material thickening in the tubing. It is prevented by "stripping" the tube free of clots. You should not attempt this on your own but should keep a diary of the amount a drain is producing. In general, if the liquid abruptly stops, there is a problem. Drain production usually tapers off gradually.

PHYSICAL THERAPY

Physical therapy is described as the remediation of impairments and disabilities and the promotion of mobility, functional ability, and quality of life. It is performed by physical therapists. This post-op modality falls under the same consideration as home healthcare providers for wound care. It can be very important because a physical therapist may identify subtle issues that indicate associated problems. Additionally, a therapist will be extremely valuable in addressing and helping you toward proper and quicker recovery and *restoration* to full function.

Medical care follows stages when a procedure is required: pre-op, operative, post-op/PACU, recovery, and eventually restoration. It doesn't end with the discharge of a patient from the hospital, yet sometimes the system's support network seems to diminish greatly or stop as soon as you leave the hospital. This is why the concept of advocacy is so important and why the new concept of restoration is probably worth more attention by the medical profession. The real marker of our success (patients and providers) should be in the restoration of the individual to function as fully as he or she did before the procedure. While certain disease processes and problems can affect that, it still should be the goal.

Although you may not be at your best during this challenging time, there is a lot you can do to take control of your course and to protect yourself as you get back to your fully restored self. Remember to be informed, be vocal, and participate in your own care.

CHAPTER 6

ABOUT DRUGS

THE DOSAGE MAKES IT EITHER A POISON OR A REMEDY

The quotation used in the chapter subtitle is attributed to Paracelsus, the German-Swiss Renaissance physician, botanist, alchemist, astrologer, and general occultist, who is also said to have first described medicine as an art rather than just a science. He believed that in order to truly practice medicine, a physician had to be more than proficient at compounding pills and plasters, because medicine dealt with the very processes of life, which must be understood before they could be guided.

In Paracelsus's day, the garden was the pharmacy. The *physick* or physician often had to be as adept at brewing and preparing his potion and cure as he was at diagnosis. Nowadays, the idea of a physician plucking a bunch of shrubs and concocting a brew for a patient to take home would be pretty outrageous. Our potions, pills, and plasters come mainly from financial behemoths, nicknamed "Big Pharma." Because of the nature of their business and their financial and social impact, they also have a great role and responsibility in our lives. It has been pointed out that they have as much of a role, meaning control, influence, and information, in our lives as do those providing our food. In some ways their size and influence are good. Pharmaceutical and biotechnology companies, such as GlaxoSmithKline, Pfizer, Johnson & Johnson, Bristol-Myers Squibb, Eli Lilly, Abbott Laboratories, AstraZeneca, Sanofi, Boehringer Ingelheim, and Genentech, a unit of the Roche Group, have the wherewithal and heft to advance cures and innovative treatments. Given that there are ongoing mergers and subsidiaries emerging, this is a far from inclusive list. As in all things, though, the good is balanced by the potential for bad. They are, after all, companies, businesses. They do take into account the costs and earnings associated with certain medications as they decide what to produce. They are not not-for-profit, and the bottom line will influence their decisions. That is not to condemn them, but such consideration is not always in your best interest.

A report published in *Science Daily* in January 2008 showed Big Pharma spent as much as 24.4 percent of total revenue on advertising in a year. That's nearly twice the amount, 13.4 percent, they spent on research and development (R&D) during the same time period. With total domestic sales of $235 billion during that same year, they spent more than $57 billion in advertising.

The Food and Drug Administration (FDA) reported 1,742 prescription drug recalls in 2009. It is estimated that 4 *billion* prescriptions were written in the United States in 2011. This amounted to earnings in excess of $290 billion according to CNN. So you can do the math.

There are whole books dedicated to the issues, merits, and concerns regarding the US pharmaceutical industry. That is not the purpose of this book, but you cannot understand the more fundamental issues of research, development, and marketing and their influence on medicines without keeping this in mind. If you are interested in reading more, I strongly suggest Jacky Law's *Big Pharma: Exposing the Global Healthcare Agenda.*

So to begin, perhaps it is best to talk about how a medication gets to you as a patient. That involves two distinct pathways: how the medication gets from the mind of the research scientist to a pharmacy's shelf (the regulatory pathway) and then how the medication gets from your physician's diagnosis and into your body (the clinical administration of a medication). To start, a few definitions are in order.

The Prescription

This term is most commonly considered as synonymous with a medical or drug prescription. However, it can also mean the care plan written by the physician, dentist, or the physician extender in a patient's chart or the directions written for a medical device or optical prescriptions for eyeglasses. This is slightly different from, but often confused with, pharmaceutical care.

Pharmaceutical care is generally defined as the provision of drug therapy and other pharmaceutical services defined by a state board rule and intended to assist in curing or preventing a disease, eliminating or reducing a patient's symptoms, or arresting or slowing a disease process. This sounds like a legal definition, and it is.

According to regulatory language in most healthcare systems, a *prescription* (Rx) is a healthcare program that governs the plan of care for an individual patient and is implemented by a qualified practitioner. A qualified practitioner might be a physician, dentist, nurse practitioner, pharmacist, psychologist, or other healthcare provider. Prescriptions may include orders to be performed by a patient, caretaker, nurse, pharmacist, therapist, or automated equipment, such as an intravenous infusion pump or a computer-driven medication administration. Think Hal, the computer in *2001: A Space Odyssey*, saying, "Why are you requesting more medicine, Dave?"

Prescriptions often include detailed instructions regarding compounding (combining or packaging) of medications, but as medications have increasingly become prepackaged manufactured products, the term "prescription" now usually refers to an order that a pharmacist dispense, and that a patient take, a certain dose or concentration of a medication at a certain interval for a certain period of time.

Prescriptions have legal implications, as they may indicate that the prescriber takes responsibility for the clinical care of the patient and in particular for monitoring individual efficacy (effectiveness) and safety. This implied agreement (a prescription is similar to a contract) also conforms to laws, depending on the type and category of substance prescribed.

Not to oversimplify, but generally this is the way it works: Your physician interviews and examines you and comes to the conclusion that you need a medication. Let's say that you've caught a cold from the person who grooms Ramon, your pet wolverine. The physician will hopefully consider any and all other medications you are taking and will generate a diagnosis (represented by the symbol Dx). Remember the SOAP note from chapter 1? The diagnosis is part of the Assessment. This will drive the Plan, the P in SOAP. The physician will then prescribe (represented by the symbol Rx) a medication as part of the overall treatment (sometimes represented by Tx) to include, rest, fluids, and so on. The prescription is also part of the plan.

If you recall, I offered a prescription for the use of this book. I'll use the same illustration to describe the elements of one you would get from your caregiver. Your physician has written your prescription, so now either it can be sent to a dispensing pharmacy or you can take it there yourself. Similar to the rules of writing an acceptably formatted prescription, the rules of dispensing are also very specific. The rules are often determined by state and local jurisdictions and are designed to maximize accountability and public safety.

For lack of a better term, a prescription is a communication mechanism between the physician and the pharmacist. It is also regulated and is a legal document. These regulations define what constitutes a prescription, the contents and format of the prescription, and how prescriptions are handled, stored, and executed by the pharmacist. Many brand-name drugs have cheaper generic drug substitutes that are therapeutically and biochemically equivalent. This means they work in the same way. Prescriptions also contain instructions about whether the prescriber will allow the pharmacist to substitute a generic version of the drug. This instruction is communicated in a number of ways.

Prescriptions often have a "label" box. When it is checked, the pharmacist is instructed to label the medication. When this box is not checked, the patient receives only the instructions for taking that specific medication and no additional information about the prescription itself.

Some prescribers further inform the patient and pharmacist by stating the indication for the medication, that is, what is being treated. This assists the pharmacist in checking for errors, as many common medications are used for multiple medical conditions and can interact. Think of this communication and the pharmacist as a safety and accountability measure personified.

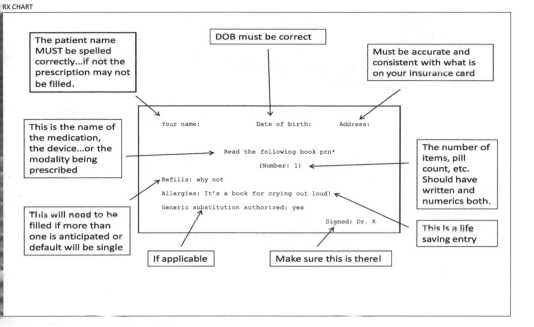

Some prescriptions will specify whether and how many "repeats" or "refills" are allowed, that is, whether the patient may obtain more of the same medication without getting a new prescription from the medical practitioner. As in the case of narcotics, regulations may restrict some types of drugs from being refilled.

In group practices, the preprinted portion of the prescription may contain multiple prescribers' names. Prescribers typically circle themselves to indicate who is prescribing or there may be a check box next to their name.

There is a lot of confusion about how a prescription must be written. Prescriptions can be handwritten on a blank template or preprinted on prescription forms that are assembled into pads. They can also be completely transcribed by hand (like on a cocktail napkin, though I don't recommend presenting too many cocktail napkin prescriptions at a pharmacy) or, alternatively, individually printed onto prescription forms. Regardless, the form must have text that identifies the document as a prescription, the name and address of the prescribing provider, and any other legal/regulatory requirement such as a registration number (e.g., Drug Enforcement Agency [DEA] number in the United States). Unique for each prescription is the name of the patient. Each prescription is also dated, as state jurisdictions place a time limit on the prescription during which it must be filled. For most states, this time limit is one year.

Within the text of a prescription there is also the specific "recipe" of the medication and the directions for taking it, including the dose per unit. Think "250 milligrams by mouth twice a day." The prescription also must include the concentration, schedule (such as "q. day," meaning once a day) and the number of units (pills, tabs, etc.).

The symbol R_x is sometimes literally translated as "R_x" or "Rx." This symbol is said to have originated in medieval manuscripts as an abbreviation of the Latin verb recipe. See? Latin . . . again.

Other folk theories about the origin of the symbol ℞ note its similarity to the eye of Horus. Or, if you are more Greek or Roman in your mythological leanings, it has been attributed to the ancient symbol for Zeus or Jupiter ♃ , the god whose protection may have been sought in medical contexts.

See, Latin yet again! Which reminds me of my favorite Latin joke . . . A man wearing a toga goes into a bar. He sits down and says to the bartender, "I'll have a martinus."

The bartender says, "Don't you mean you want a martini?"

The guy in the toga says, "No, one will be fine."

This joke always kills at the Pompeii Ramada Inn Lounge!

The word prescription, from pre- (before) and script (writing, written), refers to the fact that the prescription is an order that must be written down before a compound drug can be prepared. Those in the medical industry often call prescriptions simply "scripts."

I know it's not all that important when describing a prescription to give this little bit of background, but as you already know, I like the history of medicine. I also think it is important to know the history, because it explains the rituals, the traditional way of practicing medicine, the secret language used, and the thought process of your care providers. Knowing all that allows you a better understanding of what they are thinking and why they do what they do. That makes you better able to anticipate what is coming and better empowers you as a patient to have some control of your medical fate. And that is not a bad thing at all.

The fact that a prescription instructs someone to "take" rather than "give" is not a trivial distinction but makes clear it is directed at the patient, and is, at least theoretically, not directly an instruction to anyone else. In certain states, medical legislation has been drafted calling for distinguishing a healthcare professional's written or oral "recommendation." This would be legally distinguishable from a prescription, but since written advice to a patient is what a prescription is, that difference is hard to follow. Jurisdictions may adopt a unique statutory definition of "prescription," which is applicable as a term of art only to the operation of that statute, but the general legal definition of the word is still a broad one. In short, check with your local and state boards of pharmacy and your health departments if you have different forms being shoved at you.

DECODING THE PRESCRIPTION

In some jurisdictions, the preprinted prescription contains two signature lines: one line has "dispense as written" printed underneath; the other line has "substitution permitted" underneath. Some have a preprinted box "dispense as written" for the prescriber to check off (but this is easily checked off by anyone with access to the prescription). In other jurisdictions, the protocol is for the prescriber to handwrite one of the following phrases: "dispense as written," "DAW," "brand necessary," "do not substitute," "no substitution," "medically necessary," "do not interchange." In still other jurisdictions, the prescriber may use completely different language, as well as a different formula of words. In some jurisdictions, it is a legal requirement to include the age of a child on the prescription. For pediatric prescriptions, some advise the inclusion of the age of the child if the patient is less than 12 and the age in years and/or months is less than 5. (In general, including the age on the prescription is helpful.) Adding the weight of the child or an unusually large or small person is also helpful. In fact, truly accurate dosing is based on the weight of the individual. Think about it. Would you give the same dose to Mini Me and Shaquille O'Neal? I doubt it. Just remember what Paracelsus said, and it makes sense.

The potential abuse of narcotics, especially the controlled or "scheduled" drugs as defined by the DEA, has led to unique prescribing restrictions and requirements. A *controlled* (*scheduled*) drug is one whose use and distribution is tightly controlled because of its abuse potential or risk. Abuse potential is generally associated with drugs that produce euphoric effects or profound sedation. Controlled drugs are rated in the order of their abuse risk and placed in schedules by the DEA. The drugs with the highest abuse potential are placed in Schedule I, and those with the lowest abuse potential are in Schedule V. These schedules are commonly shown as S-I, S-II, S-III, S-IV, and S-V. Some examples of drugs in these schedules are as follows:

- Schedule I includes drugs with a high abuse risk. These drugs have *no* safe, accepted medical use in the United States. Some examples are heroin, marijuana, LSD, PCP, and crack cocaine.
- Schedule II includes drugs with a high abuse risk but also have safe and accepted medical uses in the United States. These drugs can cause severe psychological or physical dependence. Schedule II drugs include certain narcotic, stimulant, and depressant drugs. Some examples are morphine, cocaine, oxycodone (Percodan), and dextroamphetamine (Dexedrine).
- Schedule III, IV, or V includes drugs with an abuse risk less than those in Schedule II. These drugs also have safe and accepted medical uses in the United States. Schedule III, IV, or V drugs include those containing smaller amounts of certain narcotic and nonnarcotic drugs, anti-anxiety drugs, tranquilizers, sedatives, stimulants, and nonnarcotic analgesics. Some examples are acetaminophen with codeine (Tylenol No. 3), paregoric, hydrocodone with acetaminophen (Vicodin), diazepam (Valium), alprazolam (Xanax), propoxyphene (Darvon), and pentazocine (Talwin).

I might point out that, at the time of publication, there was a great deal of legislative activity related to the decriminalization and reclassification of marijuana. States can legalize a drug, but that does not affect the federal legal restriction and illegality of the drug. It only applies to state prosecution. There have been many federal attempts to reclassify marijuana, but currently it is still a Schedule I drug.

Unlike all other classes of drugs the schedule or narcotic classes require that the prescriber have a specific federal certificate and prescription pad and special type of state certificate. This is also known as a "triplicate" prescription, which is unique to this class of drugs since it requires that one of the enclosed triple copies be retained by the physician and one retained for federal accounting. This may make some difference to you as a patient, as it does require an entirely new written prescription should you need a refill or need to replace a lost prescription. It is worth noting that blank triplicates are available only from the regulating agency and are individually numbered. The accountability follows that the medical practitioner retains a copy, and the second and third copies are given to the pharmacist. The pharmacist retains the second copy, and the third copy is submitted to the regulating agency. The regulating agency can issue lists of forged prescriptions that pharmacists can check. In some cases, the prescription's validity is further limited to 72 hours from issuance. Some states are considering replacing triplicate forms with new forms that are impossible to photocopy or fax: the background is printed with repetitions of the word *void* in a color that shows up as black on a photocopy. The numbers of these types of prescriptions are monitored to identify potential abuse.

Don't lose it. Don't abuse it. And don't share it.

ABUSE AND LAW ENFORCEMENT

Forgery and falsification of narcotic prescriptions are an increasing and disturbing problem. In order to counteract this problem, jurisdictions, healthcare providers, and pharmacists are working together to take corrective actions. To make photocopying prescriptions more difficult, some medical practitioners use prescription pads that contain security measures similar to those used on bank checks. These security measures are sometimes mandated by law. Legislation also may mandate that only certain printers can print prescription pads.

Additionally, some states have increased the penalties and legal classification of theft of prescription blanks or forgery of prescriptions as criminal offenses. This allows special law enforcement treatment for these offenses. For example, New Jersey Statute 2C:21-1 makes forgery of a prescription blank a third-degree rather than fourth-degree offense.

When a forgery is suspected, a pharmacist will call the medical practitioner to verify the prescription. Forged prescriptions are not considered medical documents, so doctor-patient confidentiality rules no longer apply.

Who Is the Pharmacist?

Earlier in this book, some of the practitioners you might encounter were identified and described by the amount and type of training they had received. Of no less importance, the pharmacist is also a member of the healthcare team and may be almost as familiar with you and your medical conditions as the prescribing practitioner. In short, the pharmacist will have graduated from high school or have obtained a GED, then will graduate from a college of pharmacy with an accredited bachelor of science in pharmacy (BS) or doctor of pharmacy (Pharm D) degree. Note that a minimum of five years is required to receive the BS degree and usually six years for the Pharm D. Graduates of a foreign college of pharmacy must show that their pharmacy education meets US standards by passing the foreign pharmacy graduate equivalency exam. The pharmacist will also have completed an internship of more than 1,000 hours and must pass a licensure examination given by the State Board of Pharmacy, which includes questions about the subjects of chemistry, mathematics, pharmacy, pharmacology, practice of pharmacy, and pharmacy law.

The practice of pharmacy is more than just counting out the right amount of a drug for a prescription. Just as in many other areas of health care, the scope or practice is determined by a state regulatory board, and the board determines the scope of the practice of pharmacy. The board defines it, generally, as providing an act or service necessary for pharmaceutical care. This includes interpreting and evaluating a prescription drug order or medication order, participating in drug or device selection as authorized by law, and participating in drug administration, drug regimen review, and drug or drug-related research. Additionally, the pharmacist provides patient counseling and dispenses a prescription drug order or distributes a medication order.

The pharmacist may also compound or label a drug or device if it has not been done by a manufacturer, repackager, or distributor and will properly and safely store drugs and devices and maintain proper records for same. In many states and jurisdictions, pharmacists may also administer vaccinations. Think getting your flu shot at the pharmacy if that is okay with your healthcare provider.

As a matter of business practice, the pharmacist may write certain information right on your prescription, which he or she then keeps. Sometimes, certain information is mandated by legislation. This includes the actual manufacturer of the drug and the date the medication was dispensed. Legislation may also require the pharmacist to sign the prescription. In computerized pharmacies, all such information is printed and stapled to the prescription for record keeping. Sometimes such information is printed onto labels and the labels affixed to the prescription.

Prescriptions are usually assigned a "prescription number" (often abbreviated "Rx#" in the United States) that is unique to the pharmacy that filled the prescription. The pharmacist writes the prescription number directly on the prescription. The prescription number has the practical purpose of uniquely identifying the prescription later when it is filed either manually or electronically. The prescription number is also put on the label on the dispensed medication. The patient may be required to state the prescription number to obtain refills and submit drug insurance claims. There may also be a legal requirement for prescription numbers to be disclosed for other identification purposes, such as in regulatory investigations.

As the prescription is a legal document, some jurisdictions will mandate the archiving of the original paper prescription in the pharmacy. Often patients cannot take the original prescription with them. Some jurisdictions may entitle patients to a copy. The retention period varies but can be as long as 10 years. This is a typical requirement of all prescriptions billed to a Medicare Part D plan. Consult your local and state health department for legislation governing the archiving of prescriptions. Once the retention period has passed, privacy legislation may dictate what can be done with the original paper prescription. Legislation may also dictate what happens to the prescriptions if the pharmacy closes or is sold. For example, if the pharmacy goes out of business, the pharmacist may be required to return the prescription to the patient, to the closest adjacent pharmacy, or to the governing body for pharmacists.

Prescriptions for nonnarcotic drugs may also be "transferred" from one pharmacy to another for subsequent refills to be dispensed. The physical piece of paper that is the prescription is not actually transferred, but all the information on it is conveyed. Legislation may dictate the protocol by which the transfer occurs and whether the transfer needs to be noted on the original paper prescription.

Brand-Name and Generic Medications

This subject generates a lot of controversy, conversation, and despite all that, a lot of confusion. The same could be said for ingesting a Schedule

Similarities

According to the FDA, these are the criteria for substituting a generic for a brand-name drug:

- It must contain the same active ingredients (the chemical substance that makes the drug work).
- It must have the same dosage strength (the amount of active ingredients, e.g., 20 mg or 40 mg).
- It must be the same dosage form (i.e., it needs to be available in the same form as the original; e.g., as a liquid, pill, etc.).
- It must have the same route of administration (the way the medication is introduced into the body).
- It must deliver similar amounts of the drug to the bloodstream (i.e., it needs to deliver a comparable amount of the drug into the bloodstream within a similar time period as the brand-name drug).

I narcotic, if you think about it. The preceding chart and the following chart help illustrate the similarities and differences.

Prescription Checklist for Informed Consumers

Use the following checklist for either a brand-name or generic option to help you get the most out of your decision. If you and your doctor want to use a brand-name drug, have your doctor indicate on the prescription that it is for the brand-name drug only.

- Tell the pharmacist you want the brand-name version if your prescription doesn't specify which.

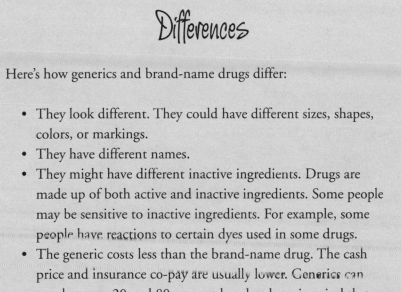

Differences

Here's how generics and brand-name drugs differ:

- They look different. They could have different sizes, shapes, colors, or markings.
- They have different names.
- They might have different inactive ingredients. Drugs are made up of both active and inactive ingredients. Some people may be sensitive to inactive ingredients. For example, some people have reactions to certain dyes used in some drugs.
- The generic costs less than the brand-name drug. The cash price and insurance co-pay are usually lower. Generics can cost between 20 and 80 percent less, but keep in mind that cost is only one factor when considering the right medication for your condition.
- Generics vary by manufacturer, which means you could receive different versions based on where you purchase your medications and what type of generic the pharmacy dispenses. Different pharmacies carry different generics. Even the same pharmacy may change generic suppliers.

- Check to make sure the medicine you get is the brand-name drug.
- To help cover the cost, ask your doctor for samples of any new drugs that you are trying.
- Ask your doctor about any coupons or voucher programs.

If you and your doctor want to use a generic drug, know the drug's brand name as well as its generic name.

- Know how to identify the generic from the label on your medicine bottle.
- Know what the generic looks like (color, size, shape, markings), especially if it looks different than it did the month before or if you use a daily or weekly pillbox.
- Check with your pharmacist to be sure that you're getting the right drug.
- Ask your doctor about any differences you might experience taking the generic.

Common Problems Associated with Pharmaceuticals

Sometimes older adults, people with disabilities, and even caregivers may face challenges when administering and taking medications. In fairness, it can happen to anyone. We get busy. We are rushing around trying to get ready for work, school, or travel, getting the kids fed, picking up our wolverine at the groomer's, and we miss a dose.

Resolving, or better yet, preventing, these problems can lead to much better results from medicines. If you have a problem that makes keeping track of your medicine or dosing schedule difficult, tell your doctor and pharmacist. Such problems include the following:

- **Memory.** Difficulty remembering to take medications. The pharmacist can provide a variety of special pillboxes or other aids that remind a person to take medications. The devices range from the low-tech, such as simple containers with compartments labeled for meals and bedtime, to high-tech, such as containers that beep when it's time for a dose, or a special bottle cap that counts openings of a prescription bottle corresponding to the day's dose. For those with severe memory impairments, caregivers are key to the proper administration of all medicines. In addition, some service organizations offer medication-reminder telephone calls for people with memory problems.

- **Vision and literacy.** Difficulty reading labels on prescription labels and over-the-counter products. Pharmacists may be able to provide prescription labels in large print. You just have to ask. Healthcare providers and caregivers can also read the information on over-the-counter products for consumers with vision impairment. Magnifying glasses or pictograms (simple picture guides) may also be helpful. Acceptable medical pictograms are approved by the United States Pharmacopeia.

- **Hearing.** Difficulty hearing instructions from healthcare professionals. Ask doctors, nurses, and pharmacists to speak louder and/or write down important information relevant to the safe use of medications. Also consider recording instructions when you are with your provider. If you ask permission beforehand, most clinicians will not mind. Caregivers or an advocate can also be "the ears" for patients with hearing impairments.

- **Dexterity.** Difficulty opening bottles, inability to break tablets, problems handling medicines such as eye drops, inhalers for asthma and other lung disease, and insulin injections. These problems are common for people with arthritis and certain types of disabilities. Large, easy-open bottle tops are available for prescription medicines. If a prescription dose is one-half tablet, the pharmacist can split the tablets for you. Caregivers are also key to assisting with the administration of eye drops, inhaled medications, injections, and other dosage forms that require fine motor skills. Again, pharmacies can provide helpful instruction sheets on administration of medicines. You just have to ask.

- **Swallowing.** Difficulty swallowing tablets or capsules. Many prescription and over-the-counter products are available in a variety of dosage forms such as a powder, liquid, or skin patch or as a suppository, greatly reducing difficulties associated with swallowing. Ask your pharmacist about alternative ingestion options, pill-grinding tools, and liquids.

- **Scheduling logistics.** Scheduling many different medications throughout the day. One of the greatest challenges for people is working medication schedules into their daily routines. Special pillboxes and other aids, described previously, can help. You might also consider signage. In chapter 3, I provided a sign for EMS. Consider making a sign or schedule to remind yourself. Timers and other obtrusive reminders are additional options. It's essential that patients and caregivers devise a plan for medication administration that fits their daily schedule. For example, mealtimes or bedtimes can be used as cues for scheduling medication if these times are regularly scheduled. Doctors and pharmacists can assist in developing a plan to best suit your daily schedule. Be sure to ask them.

Too Many Medicines

One very common problem associated with medication use among older adults and many people with disabilities is the use of multiple medications at one time. This is also referred to as "polypharmacy." Research has shown that the more medications a person takes, the greater the risk of experiencing a medication-related problem. For some patients, multiple medication use is the norm. Many chronic conditions or diseases such as diabetes, heart disease, Parkinson's disease, arthritis, incontinence, high blood pressure, pulmonary disease, osteoporosis, and Alzheimer's disease often require the use of multiple medications. In order to minimize risk, the focus must be the appropriateness, effectiveness, and safety of all prescription and over-the-counter medications. This requires excellent communication and the involvement of the patient, physician, and pharmacist. I listed the patient first because you are the biggest part of assuring that. Discuss the following with your healthcare provider.

What Is in This Stuff?

Too often patients purchase either prescription or over-the-counter medications and when asked what is in it, they shrug and give the brand name. Here is something you can do to make sure you are aware and in control of your self-administration of medicine. Somewhere on the package there will be a small listing of the ingredients. Often medications will have one or a combination of *active ingredients.* These are the chemical compounds that have the chemical or *therapeutic* effect on your body. They are the medications that you are taking for a treatment or cure. There also may be *inactive ingredients* included. You should note those, too, in case they could cause an interaction with something else you are taking.

Why is this important? Let's say you have a cold, the same one you caught from Ramon's groomer. If you are taking a cold medication that contains acetaminophen, a very common medication, and then you take a medication for aches and fever that also contains acetaminophen and then a decongestant and pain reliever combination that also contains acetaminophen . . . If you are not reading the ingredient label, you could end up accidentally taking an unhealthy or even dangerous dose of acetaminophen.

Drugs can interact in a number of ways. The basic interactions can be classified as agonistic or antagonistic. Agonism means a drug enhances or amplifies an effect. Antagonism is just what it sounds like. It's the counteraction or opposition of an effect. A drug that speeds up your heart rate is an agonist. A drug that slows your heart rate is probably an antagonist. Or by referring to the Latin, think of agony and antagonism, or as I like to refer to it, "Thanksgiving with the family."

Medications, which are drugs and sometimes poisons, as Paracelsus told us, can antagonize or counteract one another. They can amplify or enhance the effects of one another or even act synergistically. Synergy is not just amplification but can also increase and intensify a physical response or a side effect.

Hundreds of new drugs have been approved in the last 10 years. That is not a huge number, but with all of the new classes of drugs and the increase in the prescription rate in America, there is some potential for interactions that may be harmful.

An important step in preventing problems is for healthcare professionals, consumers, and caregivers to understand what a medication-related problem (MRP) is, to recognize the signs and symptoms of actual and potential MRPs, and to identify appropriate steps that can be taken to prevent these common and costly problems.

It's important to keep in mind that medication effects can directly impact or affect your daily activities. These effects or "symptoms" of MRPs may include the following. Anytime these symptoms appear, they should be considered "red flags" that an MRP may be happening.

- Excessive drowsiness
- Confusion
- Depression
- Delirium
- Insomnia
- Parkinson's-like symptoms
- Incontinence
- Sexual dysfunction

- Muscle weakness
- Loss of appetite
- Falls and fractures
- Changes in speech and memory
- A general feeling that something isn't right

ISSUES WITH UNNECESSARY MEDICATION

This MRP occurs when you are taking a medication that is unnecessary, given your current medical problems, *or* there is no longer a valid medical reason for you to use the medication. In addition, if you receive combination therapy when a single drug would be equally effective, then you may receive unnecessary medication. Patients who are exposed to unnecessary medications may experience complicated toxic effects and increased expense.

INCORRECT MEDICATIONS

This MRP occurs when you have a medical condition for which the wrong medication is taken. When you are not experiencing the intended positive outcomes from a certain medication, then you should consider that the wrong medication may have been prescribed. Other signs that you may have taken an incorrect medication include inappropriate physical reactions or a lack of response to the medication. You must have a clear understanding of what to expect—and when to expect it—when taking medications. When the result is different, the doctor should be made aware of the situation.

INSUFFICIENT DOSE

This type of MRP occurs when a patient has a medical condition for which too little of the correct medication has been prescribed or too little is taken. Medication dosages are considered too low if you have an appropriate indication for a medication, are not experiencing any side effects from the medication, yet you are not getting the desired benefit. Simply adjusting the dosage and/or dosage interval can improve the clinical outcomes, but that is up to your healthcare provider. Still, you should not hesitate to ask.

OVERDOSE

Perhaps the most common MRP occurs when the correct medication is prescribed, but the dose is too high. Based on certain medical conditions, such as kidney failure or even a patient's size, a "normal dose" of a medication can be an overdose for many people. Some medications, however, are used in the same doses for older and younger adults or even a range of weights rather than a dose per weight. Medications that act on the central nervous system (CNS) are particularly problematic because some people can be extra sensitive to the adverse effects of these medications. Examples of these types of drugs are antidepressants, sedatives, antipsychotics, and some blood pressure medications. Signs that a dose may be too high include dizziness, confusion, delirium, insomnia, Parkinson's-like symptoms, loss of appetite, falls, and changes in memory.

ADVERSE DRUG REACTIONS

Adverse drug reactions (ADRs) are a category of MRPs that can occur when a patient is receiving a medication considered to be unsafe based on these criteria:

- The characteristics of the patient
- An allergic reaction to the medication
- An interaction with another medication or food
- The incorrect administration of the medication
- A medication dosage increased or decreased too rapidly
- A side effect

Drug interactions, agonism and antagonism, can produce uncomfortable or dangerous adverse effects. They can—depending on the drug—heighten or cancel out one another's effect. Common examples of these types of interactions include blood-thinning medications combined with aspirin, or erectile dysfunction medications and nitroglycerin for angina that dangerously decrease blood pressure. Before taking any new drug, be aware of all the other drugs that can affect you, and discuss them with your healthcare provider and pharmacist.

Herbal Drugs

Most people do not realize that the sale of herbal products in the United States is largely unregulated. Companies that sell these products are also not necessarily required to demonstrate their safety and effectiveness. Some herbal ingredients are not listed on the packaging, or the listing may be incomplete or inaccurate, so you may not know what you are taking. While the compounds contained in a plant or herbal supplement may be similar or the same as a "drug," the concentration and purity may vary from plant to plant, container to container, and in other ways. Although some herbal and other natural products may be beneficial in some instances, they can also have significant and unpredictable side effects. Many herbals also interact with prescription and over-the-counter medicines. For example, ginkgo biloba, frequently used for memory loss, may interact with blood thinners, blood pressure medications, and certain pain relievers such as ibuprofen and naproxen. To avoid problems with herbal medicines, talk to your doctor or pharmacist about any herbals you use or are considering using.

WHAT YOU CAN DO

- Keep updated lists of all medicines, both for yourself and your loved ones. Keep the lists with you at all times. Include prescription drugs, over-the-counter medicines, vitamins, other nutritional products, and herbal remedies on the list. Share the lists with your doctors or the doctors of the person you are caring for.
- Store all of your medications in a designated location in your home. Keep all medications stored together in one place unless they require refrigeration or are labeled "store in a cool place." This will help if an emergency situation occurs and your doctor needs to review all your medications.
- Be sure that your medications are stored out of reach of any

children, especially if you have non-child-proof containers. If you are caring for someone with cognitive or memory problems, be sure all medications are safely stored away.

- Do not mix different medications together in one container; this will make it difficult if not impossible to identify your medications in an emergency.
- Store medicines in a cool, dry area. Do not store your medications in the medicine cabinet in the bathroom or in the kitchen because heat and moisture cause deterioration. Instead, store your medications in a designated area in your bedroom, dining room, or living room.
- Medications stored in the refrigerator should be separated from other items in the refrigerator. Consider keeping refrigerated medications in a plastic box or container in one consistent location in the refrigerator.
- Medications taken by mouth should be kept separate from items that are for external use only, such as creams and ointments.
- Expired medications (there are expiration dates on all of your medications) and any medication that your doctor has discontinued should be discarded.
- Never share or give your medications to another person.
- Some caregivers have to prepare and administer injectable medicines, such as insulin. Injections involve the use of a syringe and needle, which may be inserted under the skin or into a vein or muscle. Be certain that you understand and are comfortable with preparing the proper dosage and administering the injection. Nurses in doctor's offices and pharmacists can and should instruct you on the proper techniques for injectable medicines.

Questions about Medications for Physicians and Pharmacists

I have said this before. You can take a great deal of control of your own care by being informed and by actively engaging and questioning your healthcare provider. A good practitioner will be delighted and will welcome the dialogue with an interested and engaged patient. If the doctor doesn't—and I am sure I will take a lot of criticism from my colleagues for this—you should go elsewhere.

That said, partnership in your own medication usage isn't just your right. It's your responsibility if you want to minimize the risk of a medical mistake, misdiagnosis, or medication-related problem. To do this, you should be fully prepared for medical appointments. Before visits, write down everything you want to talk about, including important questions related to medications. Take notes during appointments, and review the notes after the appointment. Better yet, have an advocate with you. You may also have additional questions to ask of care providers and pharmacists, such as these:

- Why is this medicine prescribed?
- How does the medicine work in my body?
- How can I expect to feel once I start taking this medicine?
- How will I know that the medicine is working? Is there a typical time period after which my symptoms should improve?
- How long will I have to take the medicine? Will I need a refill when I finish this prescription?
- Will this medicine interact with other medications—prescription and nonprescription—that I am taking now?
- Should I take this medicine with food? Are there any foods or beverages I should avoid? (Grapefruit, for example, may interfere with the action of certain medications.) Is it safe to drink alcohol while on this medicine?
- Are there any activities I should avoid while taking this medicine?
- Can this medicine be chewed, crushed, dissolved, or mixed with other medicines?
- What possible problems might I experience with the medicine? How can I prevent these problems from occurring? At what point should I report problems with the medicine?
- What should I do if I miss a dose of this medicine or take too much?
- What is the cost of the medicine prescribed? Is there a less expensive alternative prescription?

- Is a generic version of this medicine available? If so, should I purchase the generic instead of the brand-name medicine?
- Do you have written information about the medicine that I can take home with me?
- Does the pharmacy provide special services such as home delivery or comprehensive medication review and counseling?

There are a number of excellent sources of information online, such as the US Food and Drug Administration website (www.fda.gov). Don't hesitate to use them.

What They Are Saying, or Are You Talking to Me?

At no other time during your encounter with the healthcare community will you feel like reciting those famous words of Travis Bickle (the Robert DeNiro character from *Taxi Driver*) than when you try to read your own prescription. If it all seems like Greek to you, it may well be . . . that or Latin. Hopefully, the insight provided earlier in this chapter will help you decode your prescription or lead you to the right people who can. Don't be too hard on your healthcare providers.

Trust me, they are not just making this stuff up for you. As you have seen, for all its supposed open-mindedness toward innovation, medicine is a very traditional pursuit. I have described the origins of the early hospitals. Since the earliest hospitals and their "pharmacies," also known as the herb garden out back, were originally in the hands of the church and the signature of an educated person was the ability to speak Latin and Greek . . . You get the idea, and we are still at it.

Another situation in which the secret language of medicine may seem forbidding is in its abbreviations. Believe it or not, there really is an organized body that gets together and decides on the approved abbreviations used in medical documentation. Participants convened at the National Summit on Medical Abbreviations in November 2004. This special one-day summit brought together representatives of approximately 50 professional societies and associations and special-interest groups to discuss medical errors related to the misuse and misinterpretation of abbreviations, acronyms, and symbols. The objective of the summit was to reach consensus on the scope and implications of this serious and complex problem and to find reasonable solutions using all of the evidence at hand and in the most dispassionate way possible.

The summit was hosted by the Joint Commission along with the American College of Physicians, American College of Surgeons, American Dental Association, American Hospital Association, American Medical Association, American Society of Health-System Pharmacists, Institute for Safe Medication Practices, and United States Pharmacopeia.

The participants supported the "do not use" list of unapproved abbreviations. Summit conclusions were posted on the Joint Commission website for public comment. During the four-week comment period, the Joint Commission received 5,227 responses, including 15,485 comments. More than 80 percent of the respondents supported the creation and adoption of a "do not use" list.

What they determined is right there on your record, even today. As you recall from the description of the SOAP note format, there are certain abbreviations that you will likely see, including these:

Hx History
Fx Fracture
Dx Diagnosis
Rx Prescription or treatment plan
Tx Treatment

How the Drug Gets to You

Now we know how a drug goes from the mind of your care provider to the pharmacist to you, but how does a drug go from the mind of a research scientist to the pharmacy? That process is a regulatory one, and the journey is complex, uncertain, and sometimes very lengthy.

According to the Food and Drug Administration, and I am paraphrasing here, companies seeking FDA approval to sell a drug in the United States must test it and pass an approval process. First, the drug company or sponsor performs laboratory and animal tests to discover how the drug works and whether it's likely to be safe and work well in humans. Next,

Table 3
Prescription abbreviations

	Latin	Meaning
aa	ana	of each
a.c.	ante cibum	before meals
ad	ad	up to
a.d.	aurio dextra	right ear
ad lib.	ad libitum	use as much as one desires; freely
admov.	admove	apply
agit	agita	stir/shake
a.l., a.s.	aurio laeva, aurio sinister	left ear
alt. h.	alternis horis	every other hour
a.m.	ante meridiem	morning, before noon
amp		ampule
amt		amount
aq	aqua	water
A.T.C.		around the clock
a.u.	auris utrae	both ears
b.i.d.	bis in die	twice daily
bis	bis	twice
B.M.		bowel movement
bol.	bolus	as a large single dose (usually intravenously)
B.S.		blood sugar
B.S.A.		body surface areas
c	cibos	food
c	cum	with (usually written with a bar above the c)
cap., caps.	capsula	capsule
cc	cum cibos	with food (but also cubic centimeter)
cf		with food
comp.		compound
cr., crm		cream
D5NS		dextrose 5% in normal saline (0.9%)
D5W		dextrose 5% solution (sometimes written D_5W)
D.A.W.		dispense as written
dc, D/C, disc		discontinue
dieb. alt.	diebus alternis	every other day

dil.		dilute
disp.		dispense
div.		divide
d.t.d.	dentur tales doses	give of such doses
D.W.		distilled water
elix.		elixir
e.m.p.	ex modo prescripto	as directed
emuls.	emulsum	emulsion
et	et	and
ex aq	ex aqua	in water
fl., fld.		fluid
ft.	fiat	make; let it be made
g		gram
gr		grain
gtt(s)	gutta(e)	drop(s)
H		hypodermic
h, hr	hora	hour
h.s.	hora somni	at bedtime
ID		intradermal
IM		intramuscular (with respect to injections)
inj.	injection	injection
IP		intraperitoneal
IV		intravenous
IVP		intravenous push
IVPB		intravenous piggyback
L.A.S.		label as such
LCD		coal tar solution
lin	linimentum	liniment
liq	liquor	solution
lot.		lotion
m, min	minimum	a minimum
M.	misce	mix
mcg		microgram
mEq		milliequivalent
mg		milligram
mist.	mistura	mix
mitte	mitte	send
mL		milliliter

nebul	nebula	a spray
N.M.T.		not more than
noct.	nocte	at night
non rep.	non repetatur	no repeats
NS; ½ F		normal saline (0.9%); half normal saline (0.45%)
N.T.E.		not to exceed
o_2		both eyes, sometimes written o$_2$
o.d.	oculus dexter	right eye
o.s.	oculus sinister	left eye
o.u.	oculus uterque	both eyes
oz		ounce
p.c.	post cibum	after meals
per	per	by or through
p.m.	post meridiem	evening or afternoon
p.o.	per os	by mouth or orally
p.r.		by rectum
prn	pro re nata	as needed
pulv.	pulvis	powder
q	quaque	every
q.a.d.	quoque alternis die	every other day
q.a.m.	quaque die ante meridiem	every day before noon
q.d.	quaque die	every day
q.h.	quaque hora	every hour
q.1h	quaque 1 hora	every 1 hour; (can replace "1" with other numbers)
q.i.d.	quater in die	four times a day
q.o.d.		every other day
qqh	quater quaque hora	every four hours
q.s.	quantum sufficiat	a sufficient quantity
R		rectal
rep., rept.	repetatur	repeats
RL, R/L		Ringer's lactate
s	sine	without (usually written with a bar on above the s)
s.a.	secundum artum	use your judgment

SC, subc, subq, subcut		subcutaneous
sig		write on label
SL		sublingually, under the tongue
sol	solution	solution
s.o.s., si op. sit	si opus sit	if there is a need
ss	semis	one-half
stat	statim	immediately
supp	suppositorium	suppository
susp		suspension
syr	syrupus	syrup
tab	tabella	tablet
tal., t	talus	such
tbsp		tablespoon
t.d.s.	ter die sumendum	three times a day
t.i.d.	ter in die	three times a day
t.i.w.		three times a week
top.		topical
T.P.N.		total parenteral nutrition
tr, tinc., tinct.		tincture
troche	trochiscus	lozenge
tsp		teaspoon
u.d., ut. dict.	ut dictum	as directed
ung.	unguentum	ointment
U.S.P.		United States Pharmacopoeia
vag		vaginally
w		with
w/o		without
X		times
Y.O.		years old

a series of tests in humans is begun to determine whether the drug is safe when used to treat a disease and whether it provides a real health benefit. The company then sends the data from these tests to prove the drug is safe and effective for its intended use to the FDA. A team of FDA physicians, statisticians, chemists, pharmacologists, and other scientists reviews the company's data and proposed labeling and instructions. If this review establishes that a drug's health benefits outweigh its known risks, the drug is approved for sale.

Over-the-counter (OTC) drugs are also regulated by FDA through OTC drug monographs, which are a kind of "recipe book" covering acceptable ingredients, doses, formulations, and labeling. Monographs will continually be updated to add additional ingredients and labeling as needed. Products conforming to a monograph may be marketed without further FDA clearance, while those that do not must undergo separate review and approval through the "New Drug Approval System."

RESEARCH

The drug research process is complicated, time-consuming, and costly, and the end result is not certain. Literally hundreds, and sometimes thousands, of chemical compounds must be made and tested to find one that can achieve the desirable result without too serious side effects. The FDA estimates that, on average, it takes eight and a half years to study and test a new drug before it is approved for the general public. That includes early laboratory and animal testing, as well as later clinical trials using human subjects.

FDA'S ROLE

According to the FDA, its role in the early stages of drug research is small. FDA physicians, scientists, and other staff review test results submitted by drug developers. The FDA determines whether the drug is safe enough to test in humans and, if so—after all human testing is completed—decides whether the drug can be sold to the public and what its label should say about directions for use, side effects, warnings, and the like.

Sometimes, scientists find the right compound quickly. More often, hundreds or even thousands must be tested. In a series of test-tube experiments called assays, compounds are added one at a time to enzymes, cell cultures, or cellular substances grown in a laboratory. Usually the process is laborious and slow.

COMPUTER MODELING

A more high-tech approach is to use computers to simulate an enzyme or other drug target and to design chemical structures that might work against it. A computer can show scientists what the receptor site (active binding site for a chemical or drug) looks like and how one might tailor a compound to block an enzyme from attaching there. Computers can give chemists clues to which compounds to make, but they don't give any final answers. Compounds made based on a computer simulation still have to be put into a biological system to see whether they work.

OTHER APPROACHES

Researchers sometimes test compounds made naturally by microscopic organisms. Those organisms include fungi, viruses, and molds, such as those that gave rise to penicillin and other antibiotics. Scientists grow the microorganisms in what they call a fermentation broth, one type of organism per broth. Sometimes, 100,000 or more broths are tested to see whether any compound made by a microorganism has a desirable effect.

CLINICAL TRIALS

Clinical trials, also known as clinical studies, test potential treatments in human volunteers to see whether the treatments should be approved for wider use in the general population. A "treatment" could be a drug, medical device, or biologic, such as a vaccine, blood product, or gene therapy. Once it has been studied in laboratory animals to determine potential toxicity, it can be tested in people. Treatments having acceptable safety profiles and showing the most promise are then moved into clinical trials.

Although "new" may imply "better," it is not known whether the potential medical treatment offers benefit to patients until clinical research on that treatment is complete. Clinical trials are an integral part of new product discovery and development and are required by the FDA before a new product can be brought to the market.

Efforts are made to control risks to clinical trial participants; however, some risk may be unavoidable because of the uncertainty inherent in research involving new medical products. It's important, therefore, that people decide whether to participate in a clinical trial only after they have a full understanding of the entire process and the risks that may be involved.

One additional word about those risks: clinical trials usually focus on "major" or relatively short-term complications or problems. There have been several instances in which an approved medication is recalled and removed from the marketplace because of the discovery of longer-term problems. It is common but also unfair to criticize the regulatory process or the FDA in such situations, because these types of problems could not have been detected during the initial trials.

They often come to light because of patients like you. So if you are taking a relatively new drug and you experience a side effect or problem, tell your healthcare provider. That way the provider can manage your problem safely and make sure the side effect is properly reported. In that way you help the system work.

Participants

Trial guidelines are developed by researchers and usually include criteria for age, sex, disease type and stage of disease, previous treatment history, and other medical conditions. Some trials focus on people with a particular illness. Some focus on a condition to be studied. Others seek healthy volunteers. Inclusion or exclusion criteria—medical or social standards used to determine whether a person may or may not be allowed to enter a clinical trial—help identify appropriate participants and help exclude those who may be put at risk by participating in a trial.

Volunteering for a clinical trial is no guarantee of acceptance or benefit. Similarly, there's no guarantee that an individual in a clinical trial will receive the drug or medical product being studied. Ask about your options, guarantees, and any other concerns. You may still decide to participate, but at least you will be informed.

How a Clinical Trial Works

Every clinical trial is carefully designed to answer certain research questions. A trial or protocol maps out what study procedures will be done, by whom, and why. Products are often tested to see how they compare to standard treatments or to no treatment.

The clinical trial team includes doctors and nurses, as well as other healthcare professionals. This team checks the health of the participant at the beginning of the trial and assesses whether that person is eligible to participate. Those found to be eligible—and who agree to participate— are given specific instructions and then monitored and carefully assessed during the trial and after it is completed.

According to the FDA,

Done at hospitals and research centers around the country, clinical trials are conducted in phases. Phase 1 trials try to determine dosing, document how a drug is metabolized and excreted, and identify acute side effects. Usually, a small number of healthy volunteers (between 20 and 80) are used in Phase 1 trials.

Phase 2 trials include more participants (about 100–300) who have the disease or condition that the product potentially could treat. In Phase 2 trials, researchers seek to gather further safety data and preliminary evidence of the drug's beneficial effects (efficacy), and they develop and refine research methods for future trials with this drug. If the Phase 2 trials indicate that the drug may be effective—and the risks are considered acceptable, given the observed efficacy and the severity of the disease—the drug moves to Phase 3.

In Phase 3 trials, the drug is studied in a larger number of people with the disease (approximately 1,000–3,000). This phase further tests the product's effectiveness, monitors side effects and, in some cases, compares the product's effects to those of a standard treatment, if one is already available. As more and more participants are tested over longer periods of time, the less common side effects are more likely to be revealed.

Sometimes, Phase 4 trials are conducted after a product is already approved and on the market to find out more about the treatment's long-term risks, benefits, and optimal use, or to test the product in different populations of people, such as children.

Phase 2 and Phase 3 clinical trials generally involve a "control" standard. In many studies, one group of volunteers will be given an experimental or "test" drug or treatment, while the control group is given either a standard treatment for the illness or an inactive pill, liquid, or powder that has no treatment value (placebo). This control group provides a basis for comparison for assessing effects of the test treatment. In some studies, the control group will receive a placebo instead of an active drug or treatment. In other cases, it is considered unethical to use placebos, particularly if an effective treatment is available. Withholding treatment (even for a short time) would subject research participants to unreasonable risks.

The treatment each trial participant receives is often decided by a process called randomization. This process can be compared to a coin toss that is done by computer. During clinical trials, no one likely knows which therapy is better, and randomization assures that treatment selection will be free of any preference a physician may have. Randomization increases the likelihood that the groups of people receiving the test drug or control are comparable at the start of the trial, enabling comparisons in health status between groups of patients who participated in the trial.

In conjunction with randomization, a feature known as blinding helps ensure that bias doesn't distort the conduct of a trial or the interpretation of its results. Single-blinding means the participant does not know whether he or she is receiving the experimental drug, an established treatment for that disease, or a placebo. In a single-blinded trial, the research team does know what the participant is receiving.

A double-blinded trial means that neither the participant nor the research team knows during the trial which participants receive the experimental drug. The patient will usually find out what he or she received at a pre-specified time in the trial.

Side Effects

Some treatments being studied can have unpleasant, or even serious, side effects. Often these are temporary and end when the treatment is stopped.

Others, however, can be permanent. Some side effects appear during treatment, and others may not show up until after the study is over. The risks depend on the treatment being studied and the health of the people participating in the trial. All known risks must be fully explained by the researchers before the trial begins. If new risk information becomes available during the trial, participants must be informed.

Informed Consent

Potential participants must receive complete information about any study. This process is known as "informed consent," and the specifics must be in writing. The informed consent process provides an opportunity for the patient to ask questions. Patients invited to enter a trial are not obligated to join but can consent to participate if they find the potential risks and benefits acceptable. A consent form must be signed by the participant prior to enrollment and before any study procedures can be performed.

Participants also have the right to leave a study at any time. Likewise, people need to know that circumstances may arise under which their participation may be terminated by the researcher, without their consent. For example, there might be a problem with the drug that is discovered during the study. Or new evidence may arise that requires alteration of the study. This can slow or even terminate the investigation.

Any reputable research project or clinical trial requires that people be given the following information:

- That the study involves research on an unproven drug, biologic (such as a vaccine, blood product, or gene therapy), or medical device
- The purpose of the research
- How long the participant will be expected to participate in the study
- What will happen in the study and which parts of the study are experimental
- Possible risks or discomforts to the participant
- Possible benefits to the participant
- Other procedures or treatments that might be advantageous to the participant instead of the treatment being studied

- That the FDA may look at study records, but the records will be kept confidential
- Whether any compensation and medical treatments are available if the participant is injured, what those treatments are, where they can be found, and who will pay for the treatment
- The person to contact with questions about the study, participants' rights, or in case the participant gets hurt
- That participation is voluntary and participants can quit the study at any time without penalty or loss of benefits to which they are otherwise entitled

Where to Get Information on Clinical Trials

Your doctor, the closest medical school, and even the newspaper often are good resources to find clinical trials. Additionally, the website ClinicalTrials.gov provides patients, family members, healthcare professionals, and members of the public easy access to information on clinical trials for a wide range of diseases and conditions. The National Institutes of Health (NIH), through its National Library of Medicine, has developed this site in collaboration with all NIH institutes and the FDA. ClinicalTrials.gov gives information about a trial's purpose, who may participate, locations, and phone numbers for more details.

Institutional Review Boards

Clinical trials are monitored and reviewed by institutional review boards (IRBs). These boards are composed of at least five members that include scientists, doctors, and laypeople, and they must approve every clinical trial taking place within their jurisdiction—usually a hospital. The purpose of an IRB review is to ensure that appropriate steps are taken to protect the rights and welfare of participants as subjects of research. If the risks to participants are found to be too great, the IRB will not approve the research, or it will specify changes that must be made before the research can be done.

IRBs also review participant inclusion and exclusion requirements to be sure that appropriate people have been identified as eligible for the trial. They often look at how and where recruitment for clinical trials will occur. IRBs review the adequacy of the informed consent document to ensure that it includes all the elements required by law.

DRUG REVIEW STEPS

In general, these are the steps in getting a new drug to the marketplace.

1. Preclinical (animal) testing is carried out.
2. An investigational new drug application (IND) is submitted that outlines what the sponsor of a new drug proposes for human testing in clinical trials
3. Phase 1 studies (typically involve 20–80 people) take place.
4. Phase 2 studies (typically involve a few dozen to about 300 people) take place.
5. Phase 3 studies (typically involve several hundred to about 3,000 people) take place.
6. The pre-NDA period, just before a new drug application (NDA) is submitted, is a common time for the FDA and drug sponsors to meet.
7. Submission of an NDA is the formal step asking the FDA to consider a drug for marketing approval.
8. After an NDA is received, the FDA has 60days to decide whether to file it so it can be reviewed.
9. If the FDA files the NDA, an FDA review team is assigned to evaluate the sponsor's research on the drug's safety and effectiveness.
10. The FDA reviews information that goes on a drug's professional labeling (information on how to use the drug).
11. The FDA inspects the facilities where the drug will be manufactured as part of the approval process.
12. FDA reviewers approve the application or issue a complete response letter.

Keeping Medications Safe at Home

One area where there seems to be a great deal of poor communication to patients has to do with the maintenance and storage of medication once the prescription is filled. Depending on the medicine, there may be any number of issues that could negatively impact the integrity and effectiveness of the drug. This could be anything from humidity, to contact with air, to sunlight.

For just that reason, specific directions regarding storage and protection will be included in the pharmacist's instructions. There are some universally accepted terms in the United States that have meaning. A list of those and what they really mean follows to help you protect the effectiveness and potency of your medication:

They are defined by the United States Pharmacopeia document 29-NF 24, which also maintains the official catalog of acceptable drug administration pictograms. Some of this is fairly technical, but many patients like knowing what the terms mean so they can handle their medications safely.

> Freezer—A place in which the temperature is maintained thermostatically between -250 and -100 °C (-13° and 14 °F).
>
> Cold—Any temperature not exceeding 8 °C (46 °F). A refrigerator is a cold place in which the temperature is maintained thermostatically between 20 and 8 °C (36 and 46 °F).
>
> Cool—Any temperature between 8° and 15 °C (46° and 59 °F). An article for which storage in a cool place is directed may, alternatively, be stored and distributed in a refrigerator, unless otherwise specified by the individual monograph.
>
> Controlled Cold Temperature—This temperature is defined as the temperature maintained thermostatically between 2° and 8 °C (36° and 46 °F) that allows for excursions in temperature between 0° and 15 °C (32 and 59 °F) that may be experienced during storage, shipping, and distribution such that the allowable calculated MKT [mean kinetic temperature] is not more than 8 °C (46 °F). Transient spikes up to 25° (77 °F) may be permitted if the manufacturer so instructs and provided that

such spikes do not exceed 24 hours unless supported by stability data or the manufacturer instructs otherwise.

(This also works for potato salad.)

Room Temperature—The temperature prevailing in a working area.

Controlled Room Temperature—A temperature maintained thermostatically that encompasses the usual and customary working environment of 20° to 25 °C (68° to 77 °F); that results in a mean kinetic temperature calculated to be not more than 25 °C; and that allows for excursions between 15° and 30 °C (59° and 86 °F) that are experienced in pharmacies, hospitals, and warehouses. Provided the mean kinetic temperature remains in the allowed range, transient spikes up to 40° are permitted as long as they do not exceed 24 hours. Spikes above 40° may be permitted if the manufacturer so instructs. Articles may be labeled for storage at "controlled room temperature" or at "up to 25°," or other wording based on the same mean kinetic temperature.

An article for which storage at Controlled Room Temperature is directed may, alternatively, be stored and distributed in a cool place, unless otherwise specified in the individual monograph or on the label.

Warm—Any temperature between 30° and 40 °C (86° and 104 °F).

Excessive Heat—Any temperature above 40 °C (104 °F).

Counterfeit Medications

In the past few years there has been a trend toward buying prescriptions online. In an understandable effort to save money and cut increasing medication costs, patients may be tempted to purchase medications outside the United States. I'd be remiss if I didn't offer some information about the risk. I'm not saying you can't or shouldn't, but the information that follows shows how risky this may be.

Counterfeit and adulterated (mixed with harmful compounds) medication is an ever-increasing problem and one that is riskier than ever due to some unsavory Internet and foreign practices that may escape regulatory pathways. According to the head of the World Health Organization's International Medical Products Anti-Counterfeiting Taskforce

(IMPACT), which works for solutions in the areas of legislative, technology, regulation, and more, anywhere from 30 to 70 percent of medications in some countries may be counterfeit. Just as alarming, products can contain the compound or drug advertised but may also contain harmful materials like ethylene glycol, which can cause severe kidney damage and death.

In some cases the temptation to pay less for the discount medications can be great, especially if the medication is in short supply or expensive. Never has a Latin term that is dear to my heart been more applicable: *Caveat emptor* (let the buyer beware).

If you feel you must purchase drugs outside the United States, talk it over with your caregiver and your pharmacist. They will have life-saving information about particularly concerning counterfeit medications.

Sharing the Responsibility

The scope and severity of problems that can occur with medication therapy are tremendous. To prevent these problems, consumers and caregivers, as well as their healthcare professionals, have a responsibility to ensure appropriate, safe, and effective medication use. All professionals involved in prescribing and dispensing—as well as the consumer and caregiver— should consider themselves essential members of the healthcare team. The consumer or caregiver who alerts his or her doctor or nurse to the need for changes to medication therapy plays a vital role in getting the best treatment.

Consumer and caregiver responsibilities center on effective communication with the healthcare team. This includes presenting actual or potential MRPs in a timely manner to healthcare professionals and participating in resolution of the problems. Before this can happen, consumers and caregivers must be able to recognize the possible signs and symptoms of an MRP. For older adults who are taking medications, any symptom should be considered an MRP until proven otherwise. When symptoms interfere with daily functioning and when the time sequence of the symptom suggests that it was caused by a medication, then a healthcare professional should be informed immediately.

Prescriptions can be intimidating and complicated when considered alone. When in the context of counterfeit materials, drug reactions, poly-pharmacy problems, and so on, they can be confusing and terrifying. Just remember. You are not alone. Consult those whom you've entrusted with your care and be a *caveat emptoring* force of your own.

CHAPTER 7

MEDICAL MISTAKES

TO ERR IS HUMAN, BUT YOU STILL NEED A LAWYER

R ecently there has been a lot of discussion about the preponderance of medical mistakes and the danger to the public. The Institute of Medicine's (IOM; part of the National Academy of Sciences) seminal study of preventable medical errors in 2004 estimated that 44,000 to 98,000 people are disabled, maimed, and die annually as a result of medical mistakes, at a cost of $29 billion. If the Centers for Disease Control and Prevention were to include preventable medical errors as a category, these conclusions would make it the sixth leading cause of death in America.

Further research has confirmed the extent of medical errors. The Congressional Budget Office (CBO) found that 181,000 severe injuries were attributable to medical negligence in 2003. The Institute for Healthcare Improvement estimates there are 15 million incidents of medical harm each year. HealthGrades, the nation's leading healthcare rating organization, found that Medicare patients who experienced a patient-safety incident had a one-in-five chance of dying as a result.

In the decade since the IOM first reported its findings about patient safety in American hospitals, many proposals for improvement have been discussed and implemented, yet the numbers do not show a significant decline. Recent research indicates that much still needs to be done. Researchers at the Harvard School of Medicine have found that even today, about 18 percent of patients in hospitals are injured during the course of their care, and many of those injuries are life threatening or even fatal. The Office of the Inspector General of the US Department of Health and Human Services found that one in seven Medicare patients is injured during hospital stays and that adverse events during the course of care contribute to the deaths of 180,000 patients every year.

Even errors that the government and private health insurers have classified as "never events," events that should never happen in a hospital, are occurring at alarming rates. Recently the Joint Commission Center on Transforming Healthcare reported that as many as 40 wrong-site, wrong-side, and wrong-patient procedures happen every week in the United States. Similarly, researchers in Colorado recently found that surgical "never" events are occurring all too frequently.

Despite these numbers, much of the American public remains unaware of just how pervasive the problem is. In some cases we may think the issues we experience are acceptable freak occurrences in patient experience, or because for the most part we want to like the people taking care of us when we are hurt and ill, we don't want to critically evaluate our caregivers. Or we may not be informed enough to know when a mistake has been made. In part, the value of this book is to make you a better consumer, a better self-advocate and partner in your own care. Again, this new informed awareness is not to create a contentious dynamic between you and a caregiver; it is to help you protect yourself and your loved ones. It is to help you navigate the healthcare environment and escape with your life, and the quality of your life intact.

In considering medical mistakes, it is important to recognize two distinct settings: the hospital or healthcare environment exclusively and those combined or hybrid environments of health care and the real world. This second environment is not included in the figures cited by the studies, so the full magnitude and prevalence of medical mistakes are not completely represented. While there is not a quantitative, definitive study addressing the hybridized environments of EMS, home health, and convalescent care and, considering the lack of many of the controls enjoyed in these environments, the numbers of medical mistakes in America may actually be much, much higher.

In a study performed at the University of Pittsburgh Medical Center, investigators attempted to measure EMS safety culture by surveying emergency medical technicians and paramedics at 21 US agencies. They used a scientifically validated survey that collected EMS worker opinions regarding six key areas: safety climate, teamwork climate, perceptions of management, working conditions, stress recognition, and job satisfaction. Safety outcomes were measured through a survey designed by EMS physician medical directors and investigators focusing on prehospital care-provider injuries, patient-care errors, and safety-compromising behavior.

The analysis of 412 surveys evaluating different areas of safety showed a relationship between individual EMS worker perceptions of the workplace safety culture and the numbers of patient and provider safety outcomes. Notably, the researchers found that 16 percent of all respondents reported that they had experienced an injury in the previous three months; 4 of every 10 reported an error or adverse event; and 89 percent reported that they had witnessed safety-compromising behavior. When respondents' outcomes were compared with their awareness of safety measures, the results were interesting. Respondents reporting injuries scored lower on five of the six areas of safety culture, while those reporting an error or adverse event scored lower for four of six, and those reporting safety-compromising behavior had lower scores for five of the six domains.

As stated earlier, measuring safety outcomes such as errors or adverse events is still particularly difficult in the EMS setting, as well as in other outpatient settings. Not to offer excuses, but there are some obvious reasons for that. EMS providers operate in unpredictable environments that require rapid interventions for patients with whom they have only brief relationships. EMS providers also often have limited access to patient medical data and risk-management resources after they have transferred the patients, which can make disclosure of errors even more difficult to identify and address. In many systems, supervising medical directors are not dedicated to full-time professional activity with the EMS. They often have full-time practices in emergency departments, with EMS direction a secondary pursuit. Because of that limited duty, they may not be able to identify or address all of the errors. This is not a criticism. It is simply a fact that makes estimating the number of mistakes in the EMS world hard to determine. In addition, out-of-hospital errors may be discovered only after the transition of care to the inpatient hospital setting occurs. There is often an impediment in getting patient outcome information back, because some providers fear that they will violate HIPAA provisions if they inform EMS. This is easily overcome. Release of information by patients and more active investigation by EMS providers to the real results of their actions are matters of public health. If EMS services don't have access to those outcomes, and many do not, self-evaluation and reporting are difficult.

The home healthcare arena is another area where the medical mistake data are probably insufficient because this environment is unsupervised and uncontrolled. This includes matters of frank medical mistakes, such as incorrect dosages by patients and providers, and increased infection-causing behavior. I mentioned infection control and hygiene risks when I addressed the hospital environment. There are signs posted all over hospitals about hand washing, and still there are slipups. Now, think about your home, and the potential for poor sterile technique is even greater. Given that properly executed sterile technique is the first line of defense in terms of infection control, you can see how these mistakes may be under-counted.

Really think about it. Imagine a home health nurse is diligently attempting to do your wound dressing change or is adjusting or examining a drain and a fly lands on the wound. It's probably not his or her fault. Just remember the last time you failed to protect an uncovered dish in the kitchen, despite your best efforts at hygiene.

This problem of medical errors and their effect on you is exacerbated by a reluctance or even fear by all providers of all calibers to mention them. Without an open acknowledgment or disclosure it is difficult to examine the problem, identify trends, and, most important, correct them. The issues associated with reporting or admitting medical errors to patients come down to two fairly fundamental human characteristics: shame and fear of reprisals.

It really shouldn't be all that shocking when you consider the causes. America is a pretty litigious place. Many people, let alone medical practitioners, fear that even if they act in good faith and communicate an error, the value of honesty will be subverted by the impulses of secondary gain via the civil courts.

As I was writing this book, I had to step away and assist a patient having a medical crisis overseas. It was the middle of the night, and as I was waiting for the call to go through, a commercial was playing on television. It was one of those hyperkinetic personal injury lawyers, imploring people to sue for a variety of offenses as he waved a fistful of money and foamed at the mouth. The guy had nicknamed himself the Whacker or the Expectorator or the Hammer of Thor or some such thing. The sound was off, but I am pretty sure the dialogue of this three-in-the-morning commercial was something like this . . .

A car crashed into a home for unwed mothers, causing calamity. Suddenly, the lawyer wearing a cowboy hat popped up on-screen. The graphic behind him identified him as the Expectorator!

The Expectorator: Hello, friends. Have you been wronged, suffered a car crash, slip and fall, dog bite, or self-inflicted act of incompetence? Then you need a lawyer. Call me, the Expectorator, and I'll get you the settlement you deserve.

A man in a neck brace and hospital gown pops up.

Man (emphatically): I drank coffee straight out of the pot and it burned me. The Expectorator got me two hundred dollars.

The Expectorator: That's right!

A woman, standing in a litter box, surrounded by cat toys, pops up holding a fistful of dollar bills.

Cat lady: I accidentally washed my hair with cat shampoo, and now all I want to eat is tuna. The Expectorator got me a thousand dollars and all these cool toys.

The Expectorator: That's right! And I can do the same for you. Call now!

Ridiculous, of course, but it does illustrate the surreal theatrics that go along with both the aggression and fear of litigation.

Compounding the legal fears are the secondary penalties associated with increasing malpractice and insurance fees that accompany an error. Thus, the culture of secrecy is reinforced. Some propose that the tort mechanism is an additional quality assurance tool, but that may not be completely accurate. The civil courts are more about individual restitution than quality control.

Interestingly enough, according to a study published in the *New England Journal of Medicine* in 1989, only *1.53 percent* of patients who were harmed by medical treatment filed malpractice claims. In 2005 the trend in payments for malpractice claims against doctors and other medical professionals was 8.9 percent, amounting to a nationwide cost of $4.6 billion, according to data compiled by the US Department of Health and Human Services. If malpractice venues were the proper mechanism for identifying and eliminating medical mistakes, then the numbers of malpractice claims would be declining. In fact, they are not.

Of no less a consideration is the issue of reputation protection. A clinician or healthcare facility that has a reputation for poor care cannot expect to maintain the respect and confidence of the community and stature among peers. No one—not a physician, a nurse, or a hospital—wants to be perceived as bad. So the willingness to disclose mistakes has a double risk and requires immense courage.

I am going to suggest again that one of the most important safeguards in the prevention of medical mistakes is in an informed and empowered patient population. So, it is important for you to know the most common mistakes so you know where to dedicate your attention and energy and when to speak up.

Top Ten Medical Mistakes

1. Treating the wrong patient or the wrong part on the right patient

This happens a lot more than the healthcare industry wants to admit.

WHAT YOU CAN DO

Consider signage or self-labeling. In medical school I had a particularly meticulous faculty member with a very common name. I'll call him "John Smith" for purposes of privacy and respect here. He was not exactly confident that he would experience the same accountability and thoroughness from his colleagues that he expected of himself, so when he was scheduled for a hemorrhoidectomy, he decided on an unconventional but memorable action. He arrived for his surgery, and when he was asked to change into a hospital gown, revealed that he had "Sharpied" himself in an attempt at self-safeguarding. He had written his name and date of birth on his chest, he said, "in order to keep someone from screwing up," but it didn't stop there.

Later when he was "asleep" in the operating room, the staff uncovered his backside only to discover that he had written a long instructive message that ran across both his buttocks. It was a long message. Both cheeks. It began, "Just a word of encouragement to my surgical colleagues . . ." When you consider that he had to have taken some time and effort to script that in reverse on that part of his body with the aid of a mirror, and then realize the same technique was employed by the genius and polymath Leonardo da Vinci . . . well, anyone functioning along the same lines as Leonardo has to be heeded! The staff got a laugh, and they were also reminded that their patient was appropriately aware of what he should expect from them.

Even if you don't go to Dr. Smith's extreme before every procedure in the hospital, make sure the staff checks your entire name, date of birth, and barcode on your wrist band. And at each handoff to a new team or introduction of a new member of the care team, insist on the same.

2. Surgical material left in a patient's body

This problem has probably existed since the beginning of surgery, or at least since the invention of surgical instruments. Although there have been attempts to minimize it—for example, by counting materials at the beginning and end of cases or employing radiolabeling (X-rayable material) into sponges and gauze—it is still an issue.

WHAT YOU CAN DO

Unfortunately, there is not a lot you can do, but if you have unexpected pain, fever, or swelling after surgery, make sure your surgeon eliminates this as a possibility.

3. Lost patients

We can track speeders, toll-road violators, and cans of peas in this country better than we can keep track of patients.

If your loved one sometimes wanders, consider a GPS tracking brace-let. Some hospitals are considering RFID (radio-frequency identification device) bracelets. This may be advisable even if you are offended by the idea of Big Brother.

4. Fake doctors

This one is hard to believe, but it is true. A recent news story in a major metropolitan area in the United States reported that a man had been con-victed of practicing medicine without a license when a patient reported that he had performed a gynecological examination in a rented storage facility. No kidding! Even more distressing, he was found to have per-formed several such examinations that had not been reported.

WHAT YOU CAN DO

If you are suspicious, contact your state medical board or board of nurs-ing. Don't just trust that the individual has been vetted by a hospital or healthcare network. Use the Internet as well. If something doesn't seem right, get a second opinion. A good doctor will welcome that. A charlatan will not. If the doctor is working out of a shipping container or an old van or panel truck, rethink your care plan!

5. Delayed care

If you have been to a hospital emergency department or doctor's office, you know that delays can occur in two ways. You have to wait to be seen once you are in the waiting area. And just getting an appointment with your doctor can seem like you are asking for an act of Congress.

WHAT YOU CAN DO

Get your physician to call ahead to the ED or to a referral doctor's office. Doctors do have leverage with one another, and a physician referral often has some level of formality and legitimacy that, unfairly, is not there when you try to make arrangements on your own. As you wait in the hospital or at the doctor's office, remember that *triage* is a word that means prioritization by need, not necessarily seniority. If you feel you are not being properly assessed or prioritized, politely ask the individual evaluating you if he understands you had, say, a spear sticking out of your chest, or a bout of really explosive diarrhea that is about to blow. It may help, but no guarantees. Just remember to speak "their" language and be as organized as you can.

6. Air bubbles

When I was a kid, I was told more times than I care to remember about the horrors of air being introduced into a vein. Then one evening when I was about 11 years old, I watched a television show about murder, and a character played by Lee Remick, I think, killed a rich relative with the dreaded instrument of death . . . a syringe full of air. It looked excruciating and sudden. Years later, when I was in medical school, I learned that the realities of an air embolus were far less dramatic in origin but every bit as harmful as mid-1970s television had led me to believe.

WHAT YOU CAN DO

In a word, participate. If a central IV line or large tube is going to be removed from your body, ask whoever is about to do it to advise you how to properly position your body. Ask what you can do to help. And if you see Lee Remick lurking in the hall . . .

7. Infections related to poor hygiene

We talked about this, but you can never be clean enough. In fact, the dream job for an obsessive-compulsive hand washer is infectious disease expert.

WHAT YOU CAN DO

Two words: Speak up! Remind them to wash. Watch for the caregiver, and I mean everyone involved on the care team—the physician, the nurse, the nurse aid, the ancillary staff—to wash upon entering your room or care environment. As pointed out earlier, this may require even more responsibility on your part in the home healthcare environment.

8. Look-alike tubes

It is surprising how often material is administered through the wrong tube or "line." This sounds idiotic, I know, and the fact that it is even a problem is pretty inconceivable. However, imagine a slightly irritating or caustic medication that has to be administered through a large central intravenous line being put into the much smaller and more fragile IV in your hand and arm, and you get the idea. Additionally, some medications or other substances require filters or should not be administered with other medications through the same IV.

WHAT YOU CAN DO

When you have tubes in you, ask the staff to trace every tube back to the point of origin so the right medicine goes to the right place. Suggest that the lines be labeled. Color coding is good too. I know it sounds like something Fisher-Price would design for a hospital, but ask the staff to color-code.

9. Too little anesthesia

Being awake while supposedly under anesthesia for surgery is potentially terrifying. While it is not common, it is a concern and something you will want to address with the nurse anesthetist or anesthesiologist.

WHAT YOU CAN DO

Ask the anesthesiologist what mechanism will be in place to assess your awareness if you will be also paralyzed while anesthetized. Just mentioning that you are concerned will be a nice reminder, and that can never hurt, which is what you want, considering we are talking about anesthesia. Get it?

10. Other mistakes

Other mistakes involve wound care, quantitative errors, and medication errors.

Wound care or progressive disease evaluation errors

This subject is all about someone, you, following the changes in a healing wound or a disease. If this person is a caregiver, great. If this person is you, you'll want to be very careful. If proper evaluation of progress or improvement cannot be made because of a lack of medical documentation or clinical notes by a caregiver, then a declining condition can become very serious before it is corrected. This is especially dangerous when different caregivers evaluate in sequence. If different people are seeing a condition on different days, you may be the only one capable of alerting someone to the changes.

WHAT YOU CAN DO

Take pictures. This is an even more self-protecting and valuable tool when you are talking about out-of-hospital or home health care. It can accurately portray the spread of a rash or deterioration or improvement of a suture line. It can show the increase in swelling of a sprain or angulation of a fracture. This is invaluable and objective. It takes away any question of accuracy of memory or other misperceptions or assumptions.

Quantitative errors

This describes the issues associated with measurement and can relate to anything from material expressed or leaking from a wound, to bleeding, to the size of something like swelling, to administration of something. Quantitative errors can also refer to measurements of things like crutches, which you definitely want right, or the size of a brace.

WHAT YOU CAN DO

The question naturally follows, Why not just rely on pictures? Pictures are helpful, but they don't always provide the full impact of scale. Therefore, it is important to also employ a tape measure. An example might be measuring the circumference of your calves in case a deep venous thrombosis is suspected or, of say, a joint following an injury. Be sure to be consistent with the unit of measurement. Use centimeters or inches for length. As described earlier, the metric system is the standard of measurement in medicine, so think milliliters, cubic centimeters (cc), liters, and so on for volume.

And finally . . . take notes. Get a small notebook and record time and date along with the volume or size. Also note if you took a picture to commemorate. Then transcribe your notes to a computer, pad, or phone application. Additionally, you should consider using a tape recorder to capture your observations, just in case.

Medication errors

We have covered the issues associated with medication-related problems. Medication administration is a complex, multistep process that encompasses prescribing, transcribing, dispensing, and administering drugs and monitoring patient response. An error can occur at any step. Although many errors arise at the prescribing stage, some are intercepted by pharmacists, nurses, or other staff. It is still worth a reminder about the "human chain" involved in getting that medication into you. Most study and attention to this subject have been hospital-centric, but the same considerations apply to home healthcare settings. Discovery and monitoring of a problem may rely on you. So it's worth some additional contemplation.

It has also been estimated that administration errors account for 26–32 percent of total medication errors. According to the landmark 2006 report "Preventing Medication Errors" from the Institute of Medicine, these errors injure 1.5 million Americans each year and cost $3.5 billion in lost productivity, wages, and additional medical expenses.

WHAT YOU CAN DO

Again, establish signage. When I see a stop sign, I stop. Why? Because the signage reminds me there is a potential for danger at an intersection. Make your own sign for yourself and others regarding allergies, special needs, and other noteworthy considerations. Write in large letters. Post it in an obvious place, next to the bed or on the dresser. You can also carry the sign provided in this book for EMS or create your own. This is even more important when you have multiple caregivers involved.

Many factors can lead to medication errors. The Institute for Safe

Medication Practices (ISMP) has identified 10 key elements with the greatest influence on medication use, noting that weaknesses in these can lead to medication errors:

1. Patient information
2. Drug information
3. Adequate communication
4. Drug packaging, labeling, and nomenclature
5. Medication storage, stock, standardization, and distribution
6. Drug device acquisition, use, and monitoring
7. Environmental factors
8. Staff education and competency
9. Patient education
10. Quality processes and risk management (less germane to you than to caregivers)

A Final Point

The purpose of this chapter—of this book—is neither to terrify you nor to create an adversarial relationship between you and your care provider but to make the relationship better informed, respectful, and efficient. That said, you should not feel constrained or intimidated because of ignorance of a setting, situation, specialty, or condition to hesitate about speaking up. It is your body, your health, and you are just being responsible.

Here's a last tip. If someone questions why you are asking all these questions, writing and photographing so much, simply say that you are taking on the task of "documentation redundancy." I'll bet you don't hear a negative word in reply.

Resources

The following websites provide accurate information about the consequences of medication errors and ways to avoid such errors.

- Drugs and Lactation Database (US National Library of Medicine): http://toxnet.nlm.nih.gov/cgi-bin/sis/htmlgen?LACT
- Epocrates electronic drug resource: www.epocrates.com
- FDA MedWatch: www.fda.gov/Safety/MedWatch/default.htm
- Institute for Safe Medication Practices: www.ismp.org
- MedlinePlus: Drugs, Supplements, and Herbal Information: www.nlm.nih.gov/medlineplus/druginformation.html
- National Coordinating Council for Medication Error Reporting and Prevention: www.nccmerp.org
- www.PrepareToDefendYourselfHealth.com

CHAPTER 8

THE BUSINESS OF MEDICINE

THE BEST THINGS IN LIFE ARE FREE, BUT I STILL NEED YOUR CO-PAY

THE NATIONAL ACADEMY OF SCIENCES

AFTER CAREFUL STUDY WE HAVE COME TO THE CONCLUSION THAT SCISSORS DOES, IN FACT, BEAT ROCK

TWO GYNECOLOGISTS WALK INTO A BAR...

Most people go into medicine because they want to help people. It's a noble principle and speaks well of their motivation. In order to do this, they study the intricacies and mysteries of the human body, the pathologies that assail it, and how to counteract them. In short, they want to save lives, improve the quality of those lives, and minimize disease, misery, and pain. It's with pain in mind that I'd like to talk about the business of medicine. It's really ironic, because after all the training and effort that a healthcare practitioner goes through, the one area that goes educationally underserved for them is the business and law of the practice of medicine.

In the past when physicians were sort of stand-alone entities, business acumen and understanding weren't such a big deal. Traditionally, physicians would adjust their fees based on their knowledge of the ability of a patient to pay. In the most primitive state, the exchange for treatment and cure would be by barter. Many years ago a country doctor could often expect payment in terms of livestock or a promise of the sale of a crop. That concept gave way to partial payment and the installment plan. In some cases a physician could waive a fee entirely.

Now, the mechanics of compensation, authorizations, co-payments, co-insurances, and healthcare underwriting is a complex, bewildering, fatiguing, and frustrating series of steps that do not always follow a logical or predictable progression. So you understand the reference to misery and pain!

At the very least, it is an additional distraction and irritation during an already stressful time. At its worst, the delay in authorization can result in a threat to life. What you are up against is that health care in the United States is big business, and it falls into a few major categories: managed care, pharmaceuticals, insurance, and medical services. To put this in perspective, table 3 illustrates the earnings of the major players in health care in 2011.

What does this mean? It represents the potential influence on public health policy and law and what recourse you as a consumer will have. Think that is not important? Look at the amount spent in lobbying efforts. During the Affordable Care Act debate, the industry spent $102.4 billion in 15 months. According to the Center for Responsive

Table 3
Healthcare EARNINGS 2013

Insurance and Managed Care		Revenues	Profits
Rank	Company	$ billions	
1	UnitedHealth Group	110.0	5.56
2	WellPoint	61.7	2.65
3	Humana	39.1	1.22
4	Aetna	36.6	1.65
5	Cigna	29.1	1.62
6	Coventry Health Care	14.1	.487
7	Health Net	11.5	.122
8	Centene	8.7	.0019
9	WellCare Health Plans	7.4	.1847
10	Molina Heathcare	6.0	.0098

Medical Facilities		Revenues	Profits
Rank	Company	$ billions	
1	HCA Holdings	36.8	1.605
2	Community Health Systems	15.0	.256
3	Tenet Healthcare	10.1	.152
4	DaVita HealthCare Partners	8.5	.536
5	Universal Health Services	7.8	.443
6	Health Management Associates	6.8	.164
7	Vanguard Health Systems	6.5	.057
8	Kindred Healthcare	6.2	—

Pharmacy and Other Services		Revenues	Profits
Rank	Company	$ billions	
1	Express Scripts Holdings	94.4	1.312
2	Quest Diagnostics	7.5	.5557
3	Omnicare	6.2	.1949
4	Laboratory Corp. of America	5.7	.583

Pharmaceuticals		Revenues	Profits
Rank	Company	$ billions	
1	Johnson & Johnson	67.2	10.853
2	Pfizer	61.2	14.57
3	Merck	47.3	6.168
4	Abbott Laboratories	39.9	5.9629
5	Eli Lilly	22.6	4.0886
6	Bristol-Myers Squibb	17.6	1.96
7	Amgen	17.3	4.345
8	Gilead Sciences	9.7	2.5916
9	Mylan	6.8	.6409
10	Allergan	5.8	1.0988
11	Biogen Idec	5.5	1.380
12	Celgene	5.5	1.4562

Medical Products and Equipment		Revenues	Profits
Rank	Company	$ billions	
1	Medtronic	16.5	3.617
2	Baxter International	14.2	2.326
3	Stryker	8.7	1.298
4	Becton Dickinson	7.9	1.1699
5	Boston Scientific	7.2	-4.068
6	St. Jude Medical	5.5	.752

Wholesalers Health Care		Revenues	Profits
Rank	Company	$ billions	
1	McKesson	122.7	1.403
2	Cardinal Health	107.6	1.069
3	AmerisourceBergen	79.7	.719
4	Henry Schein	8.9	.3881
5	Owens & Minor	8.9	.109

Politics, during 2009 and 2010, $1.06 billion was spent on lobbying, with more than $500 million spent on lobbying the issue in each year. In addition, lobbyists for 1,251 organizations disclosed that they worked on healthcare reform in 2009 and 2010, according to the center and an analysis by the Sunlight Foundation. The number of individual lobbyists who reported working on health-related legislation hit 3,154 in 2010.

Big Pharma topped the list. The Pharmaceutical Research and Manufacturers of America spent $22 million and deployed an army of no fewer than 52 lobbyists, according to the center. Blue Cross Blue Shield, which used 43 lobbyists, spent $21 million. The biotech company Amgen (AMGN, Fortune 500) employed 33 lobbyists and spent $10.2 million.

I point this out only to say that as you sit there contemplating what and how much you pay in premiums, co-pays, co-insurances, out-of-pocket, for medications, and more, it pays to have some perspective or worldview. This matters a lot. They have money and influence. What do you have? You still have a vote.

I am not suggesting you can take on this entity, but it helps to know what influences are out there when you throw up your hands in frustration and ask, "How can this happen?" As usual, it helps to know what we are talking about, or as my grandmother used to say, "Words matter." Let's start with some definitions.

Health Insurance

Health insurance insures against the risk of incurring medical expenses among individuals. By estimating the overall risk of healthcare expenses among a targeted group, an insurer can develop a routine finance structure, such as a monthly premium or payroll tax, to ensure that money is available to pay for the healthcare benefits specified in the insurance agreement. The benefit is administered by a central organization such as a government agency, private business, or not-for-profit entity.

Premium. The amount the policyholder or his or her sponsor (e.g., an employer) pays to the health plan to purchase health coverage.

Deductible. The amount that the insured must pay out-of-pocket

before the health insurer pays its share. For example, policyholders might have to pay a $500 deductible per year before any of their health care is covered by the health insurer. It may take several doctor's visits or prescription refills before the insured person reaches the deductible and the insurance company starts to pay for care. However, most policies do not apply co-pays for doctor's visits or prescriptions against your deductible.

Co-payment. The amount that the insured person must pay out-of-pocket before the health insurer pays for a particular visit or service. For example, an insured person might pay a $45 co-payment for a doctor's visit or to obtain a prescription. A co-payment must be paid each time a particular service is obtained.

Co-insurance. Instead of, or in addition to, paying a fixed amount up front (a co-payment), the co-insurance is a percentage of the total cost that an insured person may pay. For example, you might have to pay 20 percent of the cost of a surgery over and above a co-payment, and the insurance company pays the other 80 percent. If there is an upper limit on co-insurance, the policyholder could end up owing very little, or a great deal, depending on the actual costs of the services obtained.

Exclusions. Not all services are covered. The insured is generally expected to pay the full cost of noncovered services out of his own pocket. Think walkers or specially padded toilet seats, or large-handled spoons for patients who have acutely lost finer muscle control. Exclusions are often a very tricky element of a healthcare policy. They also often include conditions or situations that the insurance company deems as preexisting. As you can see, this is a very inexact and subjective process.

Out-of-pocket maximums. These are similar to coverage limits, except that in this case, the insured person's payment obligation ends when the out-of-pocket maximum is reached, and health insurance pays all further covered costs. Out-of-pocket maximums can be limited to a specific benefit category (such as prescription drugs) or can apply to all coverage provided during a specific benefit year.

Capitation. An amount paid by an insurer to a healthcare provider for which the provider agrees to treat all members of the insurer. It's an upfront payment, if you will, to cover everything a group of potential patients may need. If the patients require more care than was originally financially estimated, then the practitioner could either charge more or will lose money depending on the agreement. This is oversimplified, but you get the idea.

In-network provider. (US term) A healthcare provider on a list of providers preselected by the insurer. The insurer will offer discounted co-insurance or co-payments, or additional benefits, to a plan member to see an in-network provider. Generally, providers in the network are providers who have a contract with the insurer to accept rates further discounted from the "usual and customary" charges the insurer pays to out-of-network providers.

Prior authorization. A certification or authorization that an insurer provides prior to the provision of medical service. Obtaining an authorization means that the insurer is obligated to pay for the service, assuming it matches what was authorized. Many smaller, routine services do not require authorization.

Explanation of benefits. A document that may be sent by an insurer to a patient explaining what was covered for a medical service and how payment amount and patient responsibility amount were determined.

Generic. Usually refers to medications that are no longer under patent protection. They are generally cheaper and listed by their pharmaceutical rather than the brand name, such as acetaminophen instead of Tylenol™. Insurance will generally require a lower co-pay for these.

Formulary. A list of approved medications within a health plan that are under patent so are generally listed by both brand and generic (pharmaceutical) name. They often cost more because the drug company has less competition by still having an active patent. Being on formulary means these medications are already approved for co-pay.

Nonformulary. A medication that has not been preapproved for listing by the insurance company. The approving entity will review a prescription and either agree to pay or not or recommend another medication that it considers equivalent.

So what does this mean with regard to your bill? Let's say you decide to take a vacation, and for some reason you decide to take along your pet wolverine, Ramon. While you are driving through the country, a bee flies in through the window and stings Ramon, who in his confusion proceeds to bite you and knocks you into the steering wheel. You crash into a tree.

Fortunately, you do not need an ambulance but must see a doctor. You notice that a number of the items in your care charges are declined and you are expected to pay. The wreck itself is considered to have been associated with an existing condition: the numbness in your buttocks caused by Ramon's bite several chapters ago. You are charged for a hysterectomy that you did not get (doesn't matter if you are male or female). There is a decline for a broken kneecap and the cast you needed because you have a prior claim for a basketball injury in the ninth grade. The justification is that you could have gotten a splint instead. These are illustrations of common issues you may encounter in a medical claims case.

The medical claims case manager will want to know some things. Did the numbness cause the wreck? No, a bee did. The traffic report from law enforcement would help dispel that. Did you get a hysterectomy? No, the medical record will help eliminate that. Did the kneecap spontaneously break due to previous weakness incurred in the ninth grade? No, a letter from the treating physician may help. As for the new bite wound, as I told you earlier, maybe get a goldfish.

Absurd? Sure. Possible . . . maybe. Here is a case that is, unlike the tale of Ramon, quite real and true. I have a patient who was diagnosed with a recurrence of prostate cancer. Concerned about the potential for certain secondary problems like sexual and urinary impact following surgery, he explored his options with an oncologist. I aided him in requesting a "tumor board" review at a major university-based cancer center, and its recommendation was a less invasive radiation therapy. A tumor board is a group of specialists convened to review a patient's diagnosis and medical chart. The group then comes to a consensus opinion about the proper course of care.

In this patient's case, the insurance company declined the less invasive therapy as an option, citing it as an "experimental" modality or treatment. This is a patient who might have easily written some sections of this book probably better than I. He was informed and aware, had done his homework, and still he was being told by a form letter, no less, that he was not eligible for a fully vetted, multiple-specialty-recommended treatment plan that was also more expensive than surgery, though not by much. The insurance provider replied that its medical officer had reviewed the claim and determined that the X-ray therapy option was "experimental." There was no elaboration, and the option was declined.

This patient has a tenacious personality, and he decided that he would research the medical literature associated with his form of cancer. Backed by advice from myself, his primary-care physician, the oncologist, and the cancer center, he presented a case based on consensus medical opinion that the therapy was not only not experimental but also approved by many other insurance companies.

The insurance company responded that its medical officer was unconvinced. Meanwhile, the patient's cancer was growing. Eventually, with the advocacy of his employer and backed by the corporation's medical director, the insurance company relented. The time lost to this appellate procedure was three months.

It could have been a lethal interval. Would he have died? Probably not. Would he have had significant life impact by having to undergo a potentially comprehensive surgery? For sure. I didn't think that was okay then, and I still don't. The take-home point is that if you are going to do battle with an invisible, unknown medical "expert" at an insurance company, you had better prepare with as much advocacy as possible.

How the Bill Is Generated

It starts as your care provider writes a note in your chart, using medical terminology, and creates a differential diagnosis that includes wolverine/animal bite, motor vehicle accident, and blunt-force trauma. Additionally, the diagnosis will be fracture of . . . or sprain of . . . or contusion of . . . and *that* is how the billing mechanism is generated.

The diagnosis leads to the treatment that corresponds to a code. These codes are the Current Procedural Terminology (CPT) code, the Healthcare Common Procedure Coding System (HCPCS), and the International Classification of Diseases (ICD) 9 or 10 code. They are the mechanism by which payment is evaluated and paid for diagnosis, medical condition, and treatment. The type of classification used depends on the healthcare system, the coverage, and the patient.

Why do you care about this? When you are reviewing your bill, the code is a clue to the amount and number of specific diagnoses and determinations that add up to your overall charge.

ICD-9

The ICD codes, developed by the World Health Organization (WHO), identify your health condition, or diagnosis. ICD-9-CM (International Classification of Diseases, 9th edition, Clinical Modifications) is a set of codes used by physicians, hospitals, and allied health workers to indicate diagnosis for all patient encounters. The ICD-9-CM is the HIPAA transaction code set for diagnosis coding. If you are interested in learning more about this, feel free to get a copy of the code. I guarantee that it's a sure cure for insomnia!

ICD codes were often used in combination with the CPT codes to make sure that your health condition and the services you received match. For example, if your diagnosis is bronchitis and your doctor ordered an ankle X-ray, it is likely that the X-ray will not be paid for because it is not related to bronchitis. However, a chest X-ray is appropriate and would be reimbursed. So the documentation makes a big difference in how the medical claims case manager arrives at approval decisions.

ICD-10

This is the mechanism that the Centers for Medicare and Medicaid Services uses for establishing payment uniformity. ICD-10 codes are different from ICD-9 codes and have a completely different structure. Currently, ICD-9 codes are mostly numeric and have three to five digits. ICD-10 codes are alphanumeric and contain three to seven characters. ICD-10 is more robust and descriptive with "one-to-many" matches in some instances. Apparently that is helpful to medical claims managers. I looked at some, and frankly, it gave me a case of vertigo.

By October 2013 there was supposed to be a comprehensive transition from ICD-9 to ICD-10. Like ICD-9 codes, ICD-10 codes will be updated every year.

CPT

Physicians use CPT, published by the American Medical Association, to report medical and surgical procedures and physician service codes, rather than volume 3 of the ICD-9-CM codes. The CPT code is the mechanism the private insurance company uses to know how much to pay your doctor.

HCPCS

HCPCS is the coding system used by Medicare. Level I HCPCS codes are the same as the CPT codes from the American Medical Association.

Medicare also maintains a set of codes known as HCPCS Level II used to identify products, supplies, and services not included in the CPT codes, such as ambulance services and durable medical equipment (wheelchairs and hospital beds), prosthetics, orthotics, and supplies that are used outside your doctor's office.

How to Appeal

Appealing a claim or approval is tragically almost like a game these days. The first thing you should remember is don't automatically give up if you're denied coverage for a treatment or drug. Your medical plan document should outline what is covered and the dispute mechanism available to you. Ask your doctor's office or your employer's human resources department to get involved—they are used to dealing with insurance companies.

Remember the tenacious patient I described earlier? Get your doctor to advocate. If the issue in dispute involves specialty care, get both your doctor and the specialist to advocate. Letters matter. Make sure everything is formalized.

Keep a diary of the appeals. For phone calls, consider recording the conversations. Let them know you are doing so. They are doing it to you. Tell them it is to assure accuracy on your end.

Make notes and send documenting e-mails immediately after the call to the individual with whom you spoke. Offer that documentation if the person doesn't agree to your representation of the call. Be sure to send an e-receipt with your e-mail so there can be no claim that it was not received. This may be important for legal actions later.

One last point and this is a big one. Be nice! There is an informal game that ends when you lose your temper, use profanity, or resort to name-calling. Many years ago, I was a light heavyweight boxer. My coach and trainer told me that the one thing I could never afford to do in a fight was lose my temper. Now that sounds pretty crazy. I mean, I was in a fight, right? So the cardinal sin was to lose my temper when I got punched in the face?

Yes! As my coach said, "It's a fistfight! Did you think they weren't going to hit you? Now, keep your temper under control and your wits about you." It was good advice for a boxing match. It's great advice in dealing with an appellate process.

Medical Cards and Paperwork

Create redundancy. Copy everything, scan it, and save it, not on a computer but on an external or thumb drive. Then make backup hard copies. Check to see that they are legible. Enlarge them if necessary to make them easy to read and to limit misunderstanding. Then put them in a backup folder or envelope so that they can be produced quickly. This will protect you if your information is not readily available to the healthcare provider or system due to computer network problems, server issues, and the like.

Precare Considerations or Approvals

When going in for care, you might take certain actions to be better economically or "business" conscious. This will be important when you find that in the aftermath of the care you receive a bill that not only shocks but may be fiscally damaging in ways that you never contemplated.

We discussed trauma care earlier. Since 2002, federal law has allowed trauma centers to bill the most seriously injured patients a fee—often above and beyond an ER fee—for activating on short notice trauma personnel, such as a surgeon and anesthesiologist. This should be proportional to the services provided, but it isn't. In fact, it is an arbitrary determination often based on the mechanism by which your care is activated (EMS, etc.). If it is arbitrary, it is open to negotiation.

Hospital charges vary considerably. One report found that a routine appendectomy costs anywhere from $1,529 to $182,955, depending on which facility is used.

WHAT YOU CAN DO

- Unless it's a true emergency, try to avoid emergency rooms and use an urgent care network facility affiliated with your insurance company, or ask your doctor for recommendations. Research the hours and locations of these clinics ahead of time.

- Keep track of where all your medical bills are in the payment pipeline. If you haven't received a bill from your insurance company within 30 days, check with the company and the doctor/hospital to make sure they have correct billing information. This empowers you so that you don't immediately assume that you owe, when the insurer may still be in the process of paying.
- If your income is low, see if you qualify for Medicaid or the Children's Health Insurance Program, which provides free or low-cost health care to more than 7 million children.
- Look for billing errors. Carefully review each doctor, lab, or hospital bill, and match it against the Explanation of Benefits statement that shows how much each was reimbursed by the insurance company. Also, watch for items that may have been charged to you by mistake, such as medications, supplies, or treatments or meals you didn't receive while hospitalized or getting an outpatient procedure.
- Look for duplicate charges for a single procedure (such as X-rays, MRIs, and lab work), including those that had to be redone due to a technician's error.
- Look for charges for a full day's hospitalization when you checked out early or private room rates when you shared a suite.

The summary hospital bill you were sent probably doesn't contain many details, so ask for an itemized copy of your bill along with a copy of your medical chart and a pharmacy ledger showing which drugs you were given during your stay. You're entitled to these documents.

As I said earlier, don't automatically give up if you're denied reimbursement or payment for a treatment or drug. Your medical plan documents should outline what is covered and outline the dispute mechanism available to you. Ask your doctor's office or your employer's human resources department to get involved—they're used to dealing with insurance companies.

Don't ignore bills. If you're having difficulty paying a medical bill, don't simply ignore it. Like any other creditors, doctors and hospitals often turn unpaid bills over to collection agencies, which will wreak havoc with your credit score. Contact creditors as soon as possible, explain your situation, and ask them to set up an installment payment plan or work out a reduced rate. If paying the bill will be a hardship, speak to the hospital's billing department. Like all businesses, they realize that something is better than nothing. Offer to pay on a reasonable installment basis for a year with no interest and nothing reported to the credit bureaus. They often do this so you end with an interest-free loan and they get their money eventually.

Negotiate. Many people with no insurance discover that they're often charged much higher rates than those negotiated by insurance companies, Medicare, and Medicaid. Don't be afraid to ask for those lower rates and to work out a repayment plan—just be sure to get the agreement in writing. Most doctors and hospitals would rather accept reduced payments than have to deal with collection agencies and possibly no reimbursement at all.

Assistance programs. Ask about the hospital's patient liaison (they do exist) to review your case and see whether you qualify for financial assistance from the government, a charitable organization, or the hospital itself. These people may be social workers or administration personnel. Most providers or hospitals will forgive some or all bills for people whose income falls below a certain amount. The income levels are generally fashioned after federal poverty levels. Also pursue this avenue with your doctor or other provider—*before* they've begun collections.

If this all sounds contentious, it is. Outside the life-saving clinical issues discussed earlier, the actions you take regarding how you are "treated" financially may be the most important. Mostly, you must make sure you know how to negotiate with the care provider's office, the hospital, and the insurance company.

WHAT YOU CAN DO

- Be informed. Be informed. Be informed. There are many resources for negotiating from a knowledgeable platform. Do some comparisons for charges for similar diagnoses and procedures at other hospitals. Contact your state hospital association for tables of charges.

- Ask whether your employer offers flexible spending accounts that let you pay for eligible out-of-pocket health care and/or dependent care expenses on a pretax basis—that is, before federal, state, and Social Security taxes are deducted from your paycheck.

- Use price-comparison services like Healthcare Blue Book, OutofPocket.com, and New Choice Health to research going rates for a variety of medical services, which allows you to do your own consumer report via the Web. I would use these sources in addition to the references and tables available from state hospital associations. You want to know price ranges, and you want to know average prices for things so you can bargain intelligently.

- The government's HealthCare.gov site has tools for comparing doctors, hospitals, nursing homes, and other health providers.

The bottom line is to know what health services cost, and don't be afraid to negotiate. You'll haggle over the price of a car. Why not your health? It could be the real difference between life and death.

CHAPTER 9

THE FUTURE

HOW FOGGY IS MY CRYSTAL BALL?

AN UNHOLY PAIR O' DOCS

This may well be the most politically charged chapter of the book, and there are not a lot of "What You Can Do" sections. That will be up to you. The truth, as you have guessed, is that I have a fairly pessimistic view of the direction of medicine in the twenty-first century.

Likely, we will see the institution of great advances in technology. We already do. We are seeing the ability to have medical consultation delivered virtually anywhere there is electricity. Electronic health records may follow us in "the cloud" regardless of our maintenance of a document of our own. Surgeries utilizing robotic arms controlled by a surgeon far away are bringing capability to the most remote regions, and the surgical tools themselves create smaller incisions and promote faster healing. Diagnostic tools are becoming more sophisticated. The decoding of the human genome now allows scientists to identify the proper strategies for therapy and new cures and also to predict certain illnesses.

So why am I not optimistic beyond reason? The answer may well be found at the end of the rifled barrel of the Springfield Model 1861 rifle and can be summed up in three small words: the Minié ball. Note that I said the answer, not the resolution.

I really like history, but you have figured that out by now. What I like best about it is that the lessons of seemingly completely unrelated matters often inform each other if we are smart enough to pay attention. This is a story of war, but the application to medicine is almost startlingly direct.

Tactics and Technology: The Story of the Minié Ball Musket and the Rifled Barrel

Prior to the onset of the American Civil War, military men were trained in the "gentlemanly" process of waging war. As ridiculous as it sounds, there were almost courtly rules of what was considered appropriate behavior in sending armies to kill each other. Troops were marshaled and marched in formations originally established by Napoleon. It worked because the predictable progression of an infantry charge began with a grand march to within a stone's throw of one another (absent the artillery casualties) and then opened up in a well-choreographed musket volley followed by a finishing bayonet charge and hand-to-hand fighting. It was a brutal and terribly intimate conclusion to the conflict. It worked and, in fact, was necessary because of the poor accuracy of smooth-bore muskets, which were accurate to only about 60 feet. This approach was the prevailing school of thought in military training when the call to arms occurred between the North and South in 1861.

At the time of the American Civil War, both the North and South used a great variety of small-arms ammunition, but the type most used was the Minié ball. Ironically, tragically, in 1849 Captain Claude-Étienne Minié of France invented and perfected a new type of bullet, which bore his name, but soon became known as the minnie ball.

Prior to its invention, rifles had limited use in combat because of the difficulty in loading and accuracy. The ammunition used by rifles was the same diameter as the barrel in order for the bullet to engage the grooves of the rifled barrel. Therefore, the ball had to be forced into the barrel. This was slow and impractical and meant that rifles could be used only for one shot. If a soldier tried to reload, he would be killed by his charging opponent's bayonet before he could get another shot off. The Minié ball was subsequently improved on by manufacturers in the United States as early as 1851. Since the Minié ball was smaller than the diameter of the barrel, it could be loaded quickly by dropping the bullet down the barrel. This conical lead slug had two or three grooves and a small cavity in its base. The gases formed by the burning of powder once the trigger was pulled expanded the base of the bullet so that it engaged the rifling in the barrel. Thus, rifles could be loaded quickly and fired accurately to a distance of 200 yards.

Common sense would have said that such potential should have been recognized and tactics would change accordingly. They didn't. In fact, the battle tactics well into 1862—two years after the beginning of the conflict—still followed Napoleonic convention, and the resulting casualties of 30 and 40 percent were staggering.

So what does this have to do with health care in twenty-first-century America? Just as in the Civil War illustration, we have an incredible number of technological advances, both in the science of medicine and information technology. With proper policy, and tactical understanding, these advances could make the health and care of people unlimited. Without it, abuse and harm are completely assured.

It Is in Our Genes

Begun formally in 1990, the US Human Genome Project was a 13-year effort coordinated by the US Department of Energy and the National Institutes of Health. The project originally was planned to last 15 years, but rapid technological advances accelerated the completion date to 2003. This included identifying the 20,000–25,000 genes in human DNA, determining the sequences of the 3 billion chemical base pairs that make up human DNA, and creating a comprehensive database and library. An additional callout was assessment and attention to the ethical, legal, and social issues (ELSI) that would derive from the project. The cost of the project was $1 trillion.

An important feature of the project was the realization of the federal government's intention to transfer the technology to the private sector. This has occurred. By licensing technologies to private companies and awarding grants for innovative research, the project further stimulated the multibillion-dollar US biotechnology industry and fostered the development of new medical and medical information applications.

On May 21, 2008, President George W. Bush signed into law the Genetic Information Nondiscrimination Act (GINA), which prohibits US insurance companies and employers from discriminating on the basis of information derived from genetic tests. GINA passed both houses of Congress with a vote in the House of Representatives of 414 to 1. The Senate unanimously passed the bill after compromises were reached on areas of disagreement that had held up its passage for several months.

GINA forbids insurance companies to discriminate through reduced coverage or increased pricing and prohibits employers from making adverse employment decisions based on a person's genetic code. In addition, insurers and employers are not allowed under the law to request or demand a genetic test.

This is important as another new specialty of medicine, predictive medicine, has emerged. This specialty is relatively new and concerns the identification and applications of policy and care that may apply to predictable maladies with genetic markers. Applied correctly, this medical insight could be wonderful and life-altering. Used inappropriately, it could be exploitative and life-altering.

A 2001 study by the American Management Association showed that nearly two-thirds of major US companies required medical examinations of new hires. In addition, 14 percent conduct tests for susceptibility to workplace hazards or functional evaluations, 3 percent for breast and colon cancer, 1 percent for sickle cell anemia, and 10 percent collect information about family medical history.

You've seen how some aspects of the healthcare system influence political opinion, policy, information, and even the entitlement of care based on a variety of factors. If you have had a claim disputed or a payment initially declined only to be overturned after an arduous appeal, you understand this issue.

There are still issues that are yet to be completely determined and that will not just end with a single law. In no other area is the potential both as great and as harrowing. In order to make sure that patient interests are addressed and protected, public vigilance will be necessary as never before.

The following are issues that you might want to think about as this develops. The economic incentive to discriminate based on genetic information is likely to increase as genetic research advances and the cost of genetic testing decreases. Given the substantial gaps in state and federal protections against many forms of discrimination based on genetic information, more comprehensive federal legislation is likely needed to ensure that advances in genetic technology and research are used to address the health needs of the nation—and not to deny individuals opportunities and benefits. Federal legislation has established minimum protections that could also be supplemented and enhanced by state laws, as insurers can still potentially use genetic information in the individual market in decisions about coverage, enrollment, and premiums.

Information: It's All about You

HIPAA, implemented in 2003, sets a national standard for privacy of health information. Originally, HIPAA applied only to medical records maintained by healthcare providers, health plans, and health clearinghouses. According to the HITECH (Health Information Technology for Economic and Clinical Health Act) provisions of the American Recovery and Reinvestment Act (the Recovery Act, 2009), business associates handling such information are also held to similar standards of protecting employee medical information with a focus on electronic health records. Still, a great deal of health-related information exists *outside* healthcare facilities and the files of health plans, and thus may be beyond the reach of HIPAA. The extent of privacy protection given to your medical information often depends on where the records are located and the purpose for which the information was compiled. The laws that cover privacy of medical information vary by situation. And confidentiality is likely to be lost in some processes of insurance coverage, an employment opportunity, your application for a government benefit, or an investigation of health and safety at a worksite.

For example, your credit card account and checking transactions are likely to include information about where you go for health care and what you paid for. Insurance applications and medical claims also contain health-related information. So it is possible for such medical information to be shared among affiliates of financial institutions. Such information is *not always* protected by HIPAA.

WHAT YOU CAN DO

- Whether you have a concern or not, do an occasional accounting and request a review of your medical records from your healthcare provider.
- If you find something in error, request an amendment to your records.
- Request an accounting of disclosures of your records and to whom those disclosures were sent.

Who Is on Your Side?

It used to be your physician. Your provider operated autonomously and advocated for you when issues arose from disputable charges by a hospital, benefits or approvals were declined, and more. That is fast becoming no longer the case. As a patient you are well on the way to being less the recipient of a service and more the product processed by the system. Here's the reason.

More physicians are becoming employees. By 2014 two-thirds of physicians will work for a healthcare system or a hospital. This changes everything with regard to how the doctor is compensated, who controls the physician, and where the care provider's livelihood and loyalty will reside. This is a significant shift in the relationship between physicians and healthcare providers and hospitals. And with *you*!

Why Are These Changes Happening?

These changes are tied to the needs of both doctors and hospitals, as well as to emerging changes in how insurers and government programs pay for care. Many physicians have become frustrated with the duties involved in practice ownership, including wrangling with insurers, pushing patients for their out-of-pocket fees, and acquiring new technology. Also, the priorities of your healthcare providers have changed.

In a Merritt Hawkins Survey conducted in 2006, some 285 surveys were completed with final-year residents representing 25 different medical specialties. Of the individuals surveyed, 38 percent were in primary care, defined as family practice, internal medicine, and pediatrics; 50 percent were surgical specialists or internal medicine subspecialists; and 12 percent were hospital-based specialists such as anesthesiologists, radiologists, pathologists, hospitalists, or emergency medicine physicians. The survey showed that 91 percent preferred a salaried position with a production bonus; 98 percent expected a base salary of at least $150,000 annually; and 53 percent owed more than $50,000 upon graduation. When asked about their greatest concern upon graduating, 83 percent stated finding a job, 63 percent stated having enough leisure time, and 3 percent cited not having enough knowledge.

Of note, a survey provided to physicians over 50 years of age in 2004 found that when asked about the "dedication and work ethic of physicians coming out of training today," 64 percent responded that they found their new colleagues less dedicated than their generation. When asked about the choice of medicine as a career, 52 percent responded that they would choose another career if starting today. Some young physicians are choosing to avoid such issues as these altogether by seeking the sometimes more regular hours of salaried positions.

What Does This Mean for You?

The formerly autonomous and independent contractor, your physician, is now an employee. "Physicians" will be a salaried position dependent—just as any employee is—on the approval and evaluation of an employer for their advancement and livelihood. As a result, a great deal of the impartiality and autonomy of the physician in advocating for you and some of the traditional healthcare system checks and balances will disappear.

Additionally, the likelihood that you will be able to see a physician as a primary-care provider may be affected. Currently, discussions are ongoing about increasing the reimbursement of nurse practitioners for services traditionally provided by physician primary-care providers. Because the healthcare system employs physicians, physician assistants, and nurse practitioners, there have been proposals that nurse practitioners should be the primary-care interface, with more complex cases reserved for physician interaction. I refer you again to the chapter that describes the varying levels of educational requirements and the varying state laws that allow different levels of supervision and accountability for your determination about the appropriateness of that trend.

Hospitals as Profit Generators

A generation ago, hospitals were overseen and run by benevolent societies and charities. They did not see profit as a goal. Since the 1970s and 1980s hospital administration has moved from clinical orientation to a business emphasis. This has been due in part to laws that sought to prevent an anticipated ethical dilemma of physicians owning and running hospitals and potentially self-referring. As a result, businesspeople took charge of healthcare facilities. Businesspeople are generally interested in successful business enterprises that generate profit.

With the current shift in the greater dynamics of the health care in America, hospitals are seeking to position themselves for new methods of payment, and they are positioning themselves to become greater profit generators than ever before. This includes an emerging model known as accountable-care organizations, which is encouraged by the new federal healthcare law. These entities are supposed to save money and improve quality by better integrating patient care, with the healthcare providers sharing in the financial benefits of new efficiencies. This has the potential for hospitals to build themselves into consolidated healthcare providers, monolithic systems with a profit motivation that could be counterintuitive to the sort of ethos that patient-centric care optimization requires. In short, much of your traditional advocacy is going to be gone.

The industry has the power and soon the balance of power. The industry will have influence on billing, government, and policy, and what will you have? You'll still have the vote, and you'll still have the potential to think. It's going to be necessary—for your own well-being—that you exercise both. This kind of power-balance shift toward industry has not been seen since the Industrial Revolution of the nineteenth century. What is in your favor? Information! People in those days did not have the same access to information that is enjoyed now. The connectivity of the Web gives immediate access to information, legal actions, and thus the keys to your greatest elements of self-advocacy and empowerment. Use it.

From Recipient to Product

What is happening amounts to a paradigm shift and the convergence of three unprecedented influences in how you will be perceived by the system. The best way to describe this is as the patient changing from consumer to product. Previously you saw physicians or other care providers who determined a diagnosis and care plan based on your particular physiology and problem. They worked for you. They also processed the repayment by your insurance. They also brought "business," you, to a hospital that benefited by billing you and the insurance provider for services performed in the hospital. Hospital services are generally more costly than office-based services. The care providers answered to you. They were independent, and you were the recipient of services.

Now, with the shift of physicians and care providers working for hospitals, the dynamics of having inherent advocates will shift as well. The care provider will become a corporate employee and will seek approval and compensation from a system that values efficient processing and minimizing cost. Systems favor formulaic approaches with predictable metrics and do not take into account nuance nearly as much. Systems apply generalities. They use averages to develop algorithms and assumptions. Inevitably there will be some data points (you) that may lie outside the average.

When the process becomes the focus of something, the process *becomes* the product. That means you and the quality of your care may be less a priority than the volume of patients, the turnover and efficiencies of cost cutting, and expedited discharge. What could conceivably suffer is the quality of care and the human interaction, both of which are uniquely important aspects of proper patient care.

The philosophies are at odds. Good physicians and care providers are like good tailors. They take into account the subtleties of a person, a patient known to them. They address both the physical and the emotional aspects of care and create an environment of healing and recovery. They operate on a foundation of trust and advocacy. Administrations favor efficiencies and systems that move with predictability. Medicine and patient care are very much individualized things and are often inherently compromised by an "off-the-rack" or generalized system approach.

So the systemic structure of care, the players and their interests, and the perception of you the patient are all going through a massive change. You'll want to pay close attention and really stay informed in order to defend yourself.

Here's what I mean. I have had the horrible task of informing loved ones that a family member has died due to a trauma or acute catastrophic medical event a few times in my career. It is an awful thing to have to do, but there is something, although sad, that is far easier for the bereaved to take when it is a family you have cared for and know. Imagine that it is someone you have just met who is discussing the contingencies of end of life and resuscitation. This is the extreme case, but you see what I mean.

- Have a healthcare advocate. This may be the newest health and medical specialist to emerge. It may also be a new necessity in the healthcare arena. Here is an anecdote to illustrate what I mean and how the advocate may function.

I had a recent experience in which a friend was hospitalized. She had been suffering from a back injury and had been prescribed an opiate-based medication. Opiates affect the gut; they slow the bowel and can cause a variety of problems such as constipation or even gastrointestinal paralysis. This happened to my friend. She ended up with "GI stasis" and began experiencing severe abdominal pain. She eventually was admitted to a hospital where she was attended by a hospitalist. He did not have access to her primary-care records and immediately prescribed an opiate-based pain regimen. Unfortunately, this compounded the problem. She called me, and after some inquiry I asked to provide the information to the hospitalist. He could not be reached. The exchanges regarding the case became more strident, and fortunately alternative channels were utilized to get the point across. My friend was properly treated, and the dangerous potential of a drug-paralyzed gut or impaction was corrected, but the advocacy made the difference in avoiding some serious problems.

Although this is just one example, the need for advocacy is well supported even though how it will eventually exist is still not clear. It will probably be a hybridization of a social and legal reaction to the monolithic aspects of the restructuring care environment. Rapidly growing areas of health advocacy include advocates in clinical research settings, particularly those focused on protecting the human subjects of medical research; advocates in the many disease-specific associations, particularly those centered on genetic disorders or widespread chronic conditions; and advocates who serve clients in private practice, alone or in larger companies. This may reside in state or local governments, private settings, or as an independent business model. Only time will tell, but it's definitely worth watching. If you are interested in learning more about healthcare advocates, discuss this with your insurance provider before you are ill. You might also make inquiries to CMS or your state healthcare advocate association. State public health departments and the patient-care services department at your local hospital can give you references to private groups. As this is a pretty new player in the healthcare environment, you'll have to be your own advocate in searching for a good one.

- Consider boutique medical providers. This new trend in health care is a recent reaction by a very small section of physicians who offer their own version of a subscription service. The physician has a smaller practice and operates outside a healthcare network. He or she is sometimes retained for a small fee with individual charges for procedures and tests. It is not unreasonable to anticipate that this will become a trend, especially among patients with resources and among some businesses.

For example, perhaps you like this idea and decide to use one of these physicians. You pay a subscription fee and get your annual physicals done through the provider. If something more is required, like a CT scan or MRI, you might need additional insurance to get that service at a hospital or outpatient center, and the results would still go to your boutique physician. Your care will be more individualized, but it will cost you more potentially.

- Learn about healthcare reform. The Affordable Care Act is arguably less about health care than health insurance, including the issues of policy limitations, requirements, and mandated purchase. There are any number of texts and documents devoted to hyperanalysis of this landmark legislation, so I won't attempt a comprehensive discussion. Based on the taxation provisions of Congress, the law was upheld in its Supreme Court challenge, so the mandate of an individual's procurement of coverage will prevail. It will be important to watch the particulars of the regulations that are equally as important as the details of the law.

Patient Satisfaction: A Word of Caution

The Rolling Stones famously said, "You can't always get what you want." Personally speaking, this is a tough philosophy to accept. The seduction of "give me what I want" is almost hardwired in the American psyche. In medical care it is normal, in fact to be expected, that patients are really directed to the relief of symptoms: pain, discomfort, and dispassion. Not to show any disrespect to the Rolling Stones, but Shakespeare pointed out via Hamlet that sometimes "I must be cruel only to be kind."

What this means in medicine is that in order to be cured of a problem, you may not be able to have immediate relief. Finding out the etiology or root cause of a problem and the way to fix it properly rather than simply mask the symptoms may be a little more arduous for you. This is a really hard thing to accept when you are in pain, but there is a pretty good illustration in the classic case of appendicitis.

A patient presented to me in an ambulance with increasing abdominal pain that had come on suddenly. He wanted "morphine." He also didn't understand why I was asking questions while he suffered. Here's why I was questioning him. As it turned out, his pain had started the day before as just a general discomfort around his belly button and some mild fever. He had taken some antacids and had gotten mild relief, so he put off seeing a doctor. The next day the pain was in his lower right quadrant, and he was in incredible pain: 8 out of a maximum 10. He could not find a comfortable physical position or bear any examination of his belly.

We communicated his condition and proceeded to a hospital that had an ultrasound and a surgeon in-house. With the initial presentation and pain levels noted, he was then given some medication in the ambulance for his discomfort. Why did we wait? Had the patient's examination and complaint been altered by the medication, the severity of his problem might not have been adequately recognized. He also might have been mentally altered and might not have been as clear in relating his problem. It turned out to be the right way to approach his care. His appendix was on the verge of rupture. He was triaged appropriately by the assessing physician, and the catastrophe of peritonitis from progressive appendicitis was avoided.

Therein is an issue. When systems look for "customer" satisfaction, they may not be fully appreciative of the distinct and unique considerations of care that are counter to satisfaction.

As noted earlier, this chapter is more about possibility. We as a society stand on the verge of some significant, almost tectonic shifts in how we receive care and how much we can influence it. I'll qualify by admitting I am by nature a pessimist. It comes from a lifetime of creating differential diagnoses and addressing and eliminating the worst-case scenario. I'll offer once again the words of one more gifted, and defer to Shakespeare again via Hamlet, an even gloomier guy than myself, who put it best when he said, "For there is nothing either good or bad, but thinking makes it so."

I hope you have found this book helpful. I hope it has given you some tools to have more control and insight into your care. And most important, I hope you are better able to navigate the healthcare system and escape with your life.

Be well.

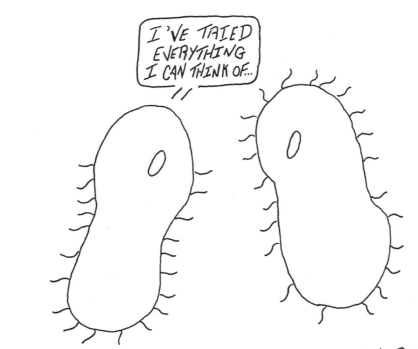

THE HEARTBREAK OF BACTERIAL PATTERN BALDNESS

REFERENCES

A.D.A.M. Medical Encyclopedia. 2013. Consumer Rights and Responsibilities: Health Care Consumer's Rights; Rights of the Health Care Consumer. 2013. *PubMed Health*. Available at http://www.ncbi.nlm.nih.gov/pubmedhealth/PMH0002672/.

Adams, D. 2004. "New Studies Back Effectiveness of Hospitalists." *American Medical News*, September 13.

AHRQ Quality Indicators—Guide to Inpatient Quality Indicators: Quality of Care in Hospitals—Volume, Mortality, and Utilization. 2004. AHRQ Publication No. 02-RO204. Rockville, MD: Agency for Healthcare Research and Quality. Available at http://www.qualityindicators.ahrq.gov/Downloads/Software/SAS/V21R4/iqi_guide_rev4.pdf.

AHRQ's Patient Safety Initiative: Building Foundations, Reducing Risk. 2003. Interim Report to the Senate Committee on Appropriations. AHRQ Publication No. 04-RG005. Rockville, MD: Agency for Healthcare Research and Quality. Available at http://www.ahrq.gov/qual/pscongrpt/.

"Aiken County Looking for Quicker EMS Response Time." 2009. Available at http://www.wrdw.com/news/politics/headlines/37299489.html.

American Academy of Pediatrics. 2008. *2007/08 AAP Medicaid Reimbursement Survey.* Elk Grove Village, IL: American Academy of Pediatrics.

Angus, D. C., M. A. Kelley, R. J. Schmitz, A. White, and J. Popovich. 2000. "Demand for Intensivists Will Outstrip Supply Starting in 2007, Leading to a 35% Shortfall by 2030." Committee on Manpower for Pulmonary and Critical Care Societies Current and Projected Workforce Requirements for Care of the Critically Ill and Patients with Pulmonary Disease: Can We Meet the Requirements of an Aging Population? *JAMA* 284:2762–70.

Ash, Joan S., Paul N. Gorman, Veena Seshadri, and William R. Hersh. 2004. "Computerized Physician Order Entry in U.S. Hospitals: Results of a 2002 Survey." *Journal of the American Medical Informatics Association* 11 (2): 95–99. doi:10.1197/jamia.M1427.

Ash, Joan S., Dean F. Sittig, Eric G. Poon, Kenneth Guappone, Emily Campbell, and Richard H. Dykstra. 2007. "The Extent and Importance of Unintended Consequences Related to Computerized Provider Order Entry." *Journal of the American Medical Informatics Association* 14 (4): 415–23.

Auerbach, A. D., R. M. Wachter, P. Katz, J. Showstack, R. B. Baron, and L. Goldman. 2002. "Implementation of a Voluntary Hospitalist Service at a Community Teaching Hospital: Improved Clinical Efficiency and Patient Outcomes." *Annals of Internal Medicine* 137 (11): 859–65.

Barker, K. N., E. A. Flynn, G. A. Pepper, D. W. Bates, and R. L. Mikeal. 2002. "Medication Errors Observed in 36 Health Care Facilities." *Archives of Internal Medicine* 162:1897–1903.

Bates, D. W., G. J. Kuperman, A. Jha, J. M. Teich, E. J. Orav, N. Ma'luf, A. Onderdonk,

R. Pugatch, D. Wybenga, J. Winkelman, T. A. Brennan, A. L. Komaroff, and M. J. Tanasijevic. 1997. "Does the Computerized Display of Charges Affect Inpatient Ancillary Test Utilization?" *Archives of Internal Medicine* 157 (21): 2501–8.

Bates, D. W., G. J. Kuperman, E. Rittenberg, J. M. Teich, J. Fiskio, N. Ma'luf, A. Onderdonk, D. Wybenga, J. Winkelman, T. A. Brennan, A. L. Komaroff, and M. Tanasijevic. 1999. "A Randomized Trial of a Computer-Based Intervention to Reduce Utilization of Redundant Laboratory Tests." *American Journal of Medicine* 106:144–50.

Bates, D. W., L. L. Leape, D. J. Cullen, N. Laird, L. A. Petersen, J. M. Teich, E. Burdick, M. Hickey, S. Kleefield, B. Shea, M. Vander Vliet, and D. L. Seger. 1999. "Effect of Computerized Physician Order Entry and a Team Intervention on Prevention of Serious Medication Errors." *JAMA* 280:1311–16.

Bates, David W., Jonathan M. Teich, Joshua Lee, Diane Seger, Gilad J. Kuperman, Nell Ma'Luf, Deborah Boyle, and Lucian Leape. 1999. "The Impact of Computerized Physician Order Entry on Medication Error Prevention." *Journal of the American Medical Informatics Association* 6 (4): 313–21.

Beaulieu, N. D. 2004. *The Business for Tobacco Cessation Programs: A Case Study of Group Health Cooperative in Seattle.* New York: Commonwealth Fund.

Beaulieu, Nancy Dean, David M. Cutler, Katherine E. Ho, Dennis Horrigan, and George Isham. 2003. *The Business Case for Diabetes Disease Management at Two Managed Care Organizations: A Case Study of HealthPartners and Independent Health Association.* New York: Commonwealth Fund.

Becher, E. C., and M. R. Chassin. 2001. "Improving Quality, Minimizing Error: Making It Happen." *Health Affairs* 20 (3): 68–81.

Benbassat, J., and M. Taragin. 2000. "Hospital Readmissions as a Measure of Quality of Health Care: Advantages and Limitations." *Archives of Internal Medicine* 160:1074–81.

Bergstrom, L. 2004. *Integrating Hospitalists into a General Internal Medicine Division.* Rochester, MN: Mayo Clinic.

Berwick, D. M. 2003. "Errors Today and Errors Tomorrow." *New England Journal of Medicine* 348: 25.

Blendon, R. J., C. M. DesRoches, M. Brodie, J. M. Benson, A. B. Rosen, E. Schneider, D. E. Altman, K. Zapert, M. J. Herrmann, and A. E. Steffenson. 2002. "Views of Practicing Physicians and the Public on Medical Errors." *New England Journal of Medicine* 347 (24): 1933–40.

Boukus, E., A. Cassil, and A. O'Malley. 2009. *A Snapshot of U.S. Physicians: Key Findings from the 2008 Health Tracking Physician Survey.* Washington, DC: Robert Wood Johnson Foundation.

Brailer, D. J. 2003. "Use and Adoption of Computer-Based Medical Records in the United States: A Review and Update." Presentation to the IOM Committee on Data Standards, January.

Brennan, John A., Jon R. Krohmer, and American College of Emergency Physicians. 2005. *Principles of EMS Systems.* Burlington, MA: Jones and Bartlett Learning.

Brennan, T. A. 2000. "The Institute of Medicine Report on Medical Errors—Could It Do Harm?" *New England Journal of Medicine* 342:1123–25.

Brown, A. 2007. "Fifty-State Survey and Analysis on Licensure Laws for Nurse Practitioners." Center for Telehealth & e-Health Law. *New England Journal of Medicine* 357: 25. Available at http://www.ctel.org/research/50%20State%20Surey%20and%20 Analysis%20on%20Licensure%20Laws%20for%20Nurse%20Practitioners.pdf.

Cannon, Christopher P., C. Michael Gibson, T. L. Costas, D. A. Shoultz, Drew Levy, W. J. French, J. M. Gore, W. D. Weaver, W. J. Rogers, and A. J. Tiefenbrunn. 2000. "Relationship of Symptom-Onset-to-Balloon Time and Door-to-Balloon Time with Mortality in Patients Undergoing Angioplasty for Acute Myocardial Infarction." *JAMA* 283 (22): 2941–47.

Carney, Patricia A., Rebecca Rdesinski, Arthur F. Blank, Mark Graham, Paul Wimmers, H. Carrie Chen, Britta Thompson, Stacey A. Jackson, Julie Foertsch, and David Hollar. 2010. "Utility of the AAMC's Graduation Questionnaire to Study Behavioral and Social Sciences Domains in Undergraduate Medical Education." *Academic Medicine* 85 (1): 169–76.

Chang, John T., Ron D. Hays, Paul G. Shekelle, Catherine H. MacLean, David H. Solomon, David B. Reuben, Carol P. Roth, Caren J. Kamberg, John Adams, Roy T. Young, and Neil S. Wenger. 2006. "Patients' Global Ratings of Their Health Care Are Not Associated with the Technical Quality of Their Care." *Annals of Internal Medicine* 144 (9): 665–72.

Chen, L., and S. Saint. 2011. "Moments in Time." *Annals of Internal Medicine* 155 (3): 194–95.

Comden, S., and J. Rosenthal. 2002. *Statewide Patient Safety Coalitions: A Status Report.* Portland, ME: National Academy for State Health Policy.

Committee on Trauma, American College of Surgeons. 2007. "Guidelines for the Operation of Burn Centers." *Journal of Burn Care & Research* 28 (1): 134-41.

Commonwealth Fund. 2004. "Promoting Hospitals' Culture of Safety: Assessing the Merits of State Adverse Event and Near-Miss Reporting." Grant to ECRI, approved November 9. Available at http://flexmonitoring.org/documents/PolicyBrief27_Patientt-Safety-Culture-CAHs.pdf.

Comprehensive Accreditation Manual for Hospitals. 2013. Oakbrook, IL: The Joint Commission on Accreditation of Healthcare Organizations.

Congressional Budget Office. 2005a. "CBO's Key Issues in Analyzing Major Health Insurance Proposals." Available at http://cbo.gov.

———. 2005b. "Fact Sheet for the CBO's 2005 Baseline: Medicare." March 8.

Cull, W. L. , G. L. Caspary, and L. M. Olson. 2008. "Many Pediatric Residents Seek and Obtain Part-Time Positions." *Pediatrics* 121 (2): 276–81.

Cunningham, P., and J. May. 2009. *Medicaid Patients Increasingly Concentrated among Physicians: Tracking Report No. 16.* Available at http://www.ncbi.nlm.nih.gov/pubmed/16918046.

Davis, K., Stephen C. Schoenbaum, Karen Scott Collins, Katie Tenney, Dora L. Hughes, and Anne-Marie J. Audet. 2002. *Room for Improvement: Patients Report on the Quality of Their Health Care.* New York: Commonwealth Fund.

Dexter, P. R., Susan Perkins, J. Marc Overhage, Kati Maharry, Richard B. Kohler, and Clement J. McDonald. 2001. "A Computerized Reminder System to Increase the Use of Preventive Care for Hospitalized Patients." *New England Journal of Medicine* 345: 965–70.

Dick, W. F. 2003. "Anglo-American vs. Franco-German Emergency Medical Services System." *Prehospital and Disaster Medicine* 18 (1): 29–35; discussion 35–37.

Feinbloom, David, and Joseph Min Wah Li. 2006. "The SHM 2005–2006 Survey: The Authoritative Source on the State of the Hospitalist Movement." *Medscape.* Available at http://www.medscape.org/viewarticle/536060.

Fenton, Joshua J., Anthony F. Jerant, Klea D. Bertakis, and Peter Franks. 2012. "The Cost of Satisfaction: A National Study of Patient Satisfaction, Health Care Utilization, Expenditures, and Mortality." *Archives of Internal Medicine* 172 (5): 405–11.

Findlay, S., ed. 2000. *Reducing Medical Errors and Improving Patient Safety: Success from the Front Lines of Medicine.* Washington, DC: National Coalition on Health Care and Institute for Healthcare Improvement.

Finkelstein, J. B. 2004. "Senate Passes Patient Safety Bill with New Error Reporting System." August, amednews.com. Available at http://www.amednews.com/article/20040809/government/308099983/1/.

Flint, S. S. 2006. "Ensuring Equal Access for Medicaid Children." *Health and Social Work* 31 (1): 65–71.

Gallagher, T. H., A. D. Waterman, A. G. Ebers, V. J. Fraser, and W. Levinson. 2003. "Patients' and Physicians' Attitudes regarding the Disclosure of Medical Records." *JAMA* 289 (8): 1001–7.

Galvin, R. S. 2001. "The Business Case for Quality." *Health Affairs* 20 (6): 57–59.

Gaston, S. R. 1971. "Accidental Death and Disability: The Neglected Disease of Modern Society. A Progress Report." *Journal of Trauma* 11 (3): 195–206.

Genetic Alliance: GINA Coverage THOMAS: HR 493 Genetic Information Non-discrimination Act of 2007. Available at http://thomas.loc.gov/cgi-bin/query/z?c110:H.R.493:.

Genetic Information Nondiscrimination Act of 2008 (Public Law 110–233). H.R. 493, 110th Cong. Available at http://web.ornl.gov/sci/techresources/Human_Genome/publicat/GINAMay2008.pdf.

Gever, John, ed. 2011. "Hospitalist Care More Costly on Balance." Available at http://www.medpagetoday.com/HospitalBasedMedicine/Hospitalists/27861.

Goldstein, J. 2008. "As Doctors Get a Life, Strain Shows." *Wall Street Journal*, April 29, A18.

GQ Medical School Graduation Questionnaire: All Schools Summary Report. Final. 2010. Association of American Medical Colleges. Available at https://www.aamc.org/download/140716/data/.

Gurwitz, J. H., T. S. Field, J. Avorn, D. McCormick, S. Jain, M. Eckler, M. Benser, A. C. Edmondson, and D. W. Bates. 2000. "Incidence and Preventability of Adverse Drug Events in Nursing Homes." *American Journal of Medicine* 109 (2): 87–94.

Gurwitz, J. H., T. S. Field, L. R. Harrold, J. Rothschild, K. Debellis, A. C. Seger, C. Cadoret, L. S. Fish, L. Garber, M. Kelleher, and D. W. Bates. 2003. "Incidence and Preventability of Adverse Drug Events among Older Persons in the Ambulatory Setting." *JAMA* 289 (9): 1107–16.

Hayward, R. A., and T. P. Hofer. 2001. "Estimating Hospital Deaths Due to Medical Errors: Preventability Is in the Eye of the Reviewer." *JAMA* 286 (4): 415–20.

"Health Market Changes Spur Use of Hospitalists across the U.S." 2005. Press release, Center for Studying Health System Change. February 1. Available at http://www.hschange.org/CONTENT/729/.

"Health Policy Brief: Nurse Practitioners and Primary Care." 2012. *Health Affairs*, October 25.

Hibbard, J., and J. J. Jewett. 1996. "What Type of Information Do Consumers Want in a Health Care Report Card?" *Medical Care Research and Review* 53 (1): 28–47.

Hofer, T. P., and R. A. Hayward. 1995. "Can Early Re-admission Rates Accurately Detect Poor Quality Hospitals?" *Medical Care* 33: 234–45.

———. 1996. "Identifying Poor-Quality Hospitals: Can Hospital Mortality Rates Detect Quality Problems for Medical Diagnoses?" *Medical Care* 34: 737–53.

Huddleston, J. M., K. H. Long, J. M. Naessens, D. Vanness, D. Larson, R. Trousdale, M. Plevak, M. Cabanela, D. Ilstrup, and R. M. Wachter. 2004. "Medical and Surgical Comanagement after Elective Hip and Knee Arthroplasty: A Randomized Controlled Trial." *Annals of Internal Medicine* 141: 28–38.

The Impact of the National Drug Shortage on Emergency Care Proceedings Report. 2012. Washington, DC: Emergency Care Coordination Center, Assistant Secretary Preparedness and Response, US DHHS.

The Impending Collapse of Primary Care Medicine and Its Implications for the State of the Nation's Health Care: A Report from the American College of Physicians. 2006. Available at http://www.providersedge.com/ehdocs/ehr_articles/The_Impending_Collapse_of_Primary_Care_Medicine_and_Its_Implications_for_the_State_of_the_Nation-s_Healthcare.pdf.

Institute for Safe Medication Practices. 2011. *2011 ISMP Medication Safety Self Assessment for Hospitals.* Available at http://www.ismp.org/selfassessments/hospital/2011/pdfs.asp.

Institute of Medicine. 1999. *To Err Is Human: Building a Safer Health Care System.* Washington, DC: National Academies Press.

———. 2003. *Fostering Rapid Advances in Health Care: Learning from System Demonstrations.* Washington, DC: National Academies Press.

———. 2004. *Patient Safety: Achieving a New Standard for Care.* Washington, DC: National Academies Press.

Institute of Medicine Committee on Quality of Health Care in America. 2001. *Crossing the Quality Chasm: A New Health System for the 21st Century.* Quality Chasm Series. Washington, DC: National Academies Press.

Jencks, S. 2000. "Public Reporting of Serious Medical Errors." *Effective Clinical Practice* 3: 299–301.

Joint Commission on Accreditation of Healthcare Organizations. 2013a. *Facts about Patient Safety.* Available at http://www.jointcommission.org/assets/1/18/Patient_Safety.pdf.

———. 2013b. *National Patient Safety Goals.* Available at http://www.jointcommission.org/standards_information/npsgs.aspx.

Kachalia, A., and D. M. Studdert. 2004. "Professional Liability Issues in Graduate Medical Education." *JAMA* 292 (9): 1051–56.

Kaiser Family Foundation, Agency for Healthcare Quality and Research, and the Harvard School of Public Health. 2004. *National Survey on Consumers' Experiences with Patient Safety and Quality Information.* News release, November 17. Available at http://kff.org/health-costs/poll-finding/national-survey-on-consumers-experiences-with-patient/.

Kavilanz, Parija. 2012. "Demise of the Solo Doctor." *CNNMoney,* July 11.

Klein, M. B., C. B. Kramer, J. Nelson, F. P. Rivara, N. S. Gibran, and T. Concannon. 2009. "Geographic Access to Burn Center Hospitals." *JAMA* 302 (16): 1774–81.

Kralovec, P., J. A. Miller, L. Wellikson, and J. M. Huddleston. 2006. "The Status of Hospital Medicine Groups in the United States." *Journal of Hospital Medicine* 1 (2): 75–80.

Kuehl, Alexander. 2002. *Prehospital Systems and Medical Oversight.* Dubuque, IA: Kendall Hunt Publishing.

Kuo, Y.-F., and J. S. Goodwin. 2011. "Association of Hospitalist Care with Medical Utilization after Discharge: Evidence of Cost Shift from a Cohort Study." *Annals of Internal Medicine* 155: 152–59.

Kuperman, G. J. 2003. "Computer Physician Order Entry: Benefits, Costs and Issues." *Annals of Internal Medicine* 139: 31–39.

Lamb, Rae M., David M. Studdert, Richard M. J. Bohmer, Donald M. Berwick, and Troyen A. Brennan. 2003. "Hospital Disclosure Practices: Results of a National Survey." *Health Affairs* 22: 73–83.

Leape, L. L. 2000. "IOM Medical Error Figures Are Not Exaggerated." *JAMA* 284 (1): 95–97.

———. 2004. "Learning from Mistakes: Toward Error-Free Medicine." Investigator Awards in Health Policy. *Research in Profile* 11: 1–4.

Leatherman, Sheila, and Douglas McCarthy. 2002. *Quality of Health Care in the United States: A Chartbook.* New York: Commonwealth Fund.

Lindenauer, P. K., M. B. Rothberg, P. S. Pekow, C. Kenwood, E. M. Benjamin, and A. D. Auerbach. 2007. "Outcomes of Care by Hospitalists, General Internists, and Family Physicians." *New England Journal of Medicine* 357: 2589–2600.

Ludwig, Gary G. 2004. "EMS Response Time Standards." EMS World, April 1. Available at http://publicsafety.com/article/article.jsp?id=2255&siteSection=5.

Lurie, J. D., D. P. Miller, P. K. Lindenauer, R. M. Wachter, and H. C. Sox. 1999. "The Potential Size of the Hospitalist Workforce in the United States." *American Journal of Medicine* 106: 441–45.

Maio, V., N. Goldfarb, C. Carter, and D. Nash. 2003. *Value-Based Purchasing: A Review of the Literature.* New York: Commonwealth Fund.

Making Health Care Safer: A Critical Analysis of Patient Safety Practices. 2001. Evidence Report / Technology Assessment no. 43. Rockville, MD: Agency for Healthcare Research and Quality.

Margolis, P. A., R. L. Cook, J. A. Earp, C. M. Lannon, L. L. Keyes, and J. D. Klein. 1992. "Factors Associated with Pediatricians' Participation in Medicaid in North Carolina." *JAMA* 267 (14): 1942–46.

Mathews, A. W. 2010. "When the Doctor Has a Boss: More Physicians Are Going to Work for Hospitals Rather Than Hanging a Shingle." *Wall Street Journal*, November 8. Available at http://online.wsj.com/article/SB10001424052748703856504575600412716683130.html.html.

McGlynn, Elizabeth A., Steven M. Asch, John Adams, Joan Keesey, Jennifer Hicks, Alison DeCristofaro, and Eve A. Kerr. 2003. "The Quality of Health Care Delivered to Adults in the United States." *New England Journal of Medicine* 348 (26): 2635–45.

"MDPH Creates a New Patient Center to Reduce Medical Errors." 2004. Available at http://www.mass.gov.

Meltzer, D., W. G. Manning, J. Morrison, N. S. Manish, T. Jin, T. Guth, and W. Levinson. 2002. "Effects of Physician Experience on Cost and Outcomes on an Academic General Medicine Service: Results of a Trial of Hospitalists." *Annals of Internal Medicine* 137 (11): 866–74.

Merritt Hawkins & Associates. 2006. *Summary Report: 2006 Survey of Final Year Medical Residents.* Available at http://www.merritthawkins.com/pdf/mha2006residentsurvey.pdf.

Meyer, J. A. 2004. *Hospital Quality: Ingredients for Success—Overview and Lessons Learned.* New York: Commonwealth Fund.

Midwest Business Group Health (MBGH). 2002. *Reducing the Costs of Poor-Quality Health Care through Responsible Purchasing Leadership.* Chicago: MGBH.

Millenson, M. L. 2003. "The Silence." *Health Affairs* 22 (2): 103–4.

Miller, J. A., ed. 2005. *How Hospitalists Add Value. Special Supplement to The Hospitalist* 9 (Supplement 1). New York: Wiley.

Milstein, A. 1999. "An Employer's Perspective on Hospitalists as a Source of Improved Health Care Value." *Annals of Internal Medicine* 130: 36–42.

National Conference of State Legislatures. *Genetic Privacy Laws* [50-state breakdown]. 2008. Available at http://www.ncsl.org/issues-research/health/genetic-privacy-laws.aspx.

National Fire Protection Association. 2010a. *NFPA 1710: Standard for the Organization and Deployment of Fire Suppression Operations, Emergency Medical Operations, and Special Operations to the Public by Career Fire Departments.* Available at http://www.nfpa.org/codes-and-standards/standards-development-process/safer-act-grant/nfpa-1710.

———. 2010b. *NFPA 1720: Standard for the Organization and Deployment of Fire Suppression Operations, Emergency Medical Operations and Special Operations to the Public by Volunteer Fire Departments.* Available at http://www.nfpa.org/codes-and-standards/standards-development-process/safer-act-grant/nfpa-1720.

Newhouse, J. P. 2002. "Why Is There a Quality Chasm?" *Health Affairs* 21 (4): 13–26.

Parekh, V., S. Saint, S. Furney, S. Kaufman, and L. McMahon. 2004. "What Effect Does Inpatient Physician Specialty and Experience Have on Clinical Outcomes and Resource Utilization on a General Medicine Service?" *Journal of General Internal Medicine* 19: 395–401.

Patient Safety Task Force Fact Sheet. Rockville, MD: Agency for Healthcare Research and Quality. Available at http://www.premierinc.com/all/safety/resources/patient_safety/downloads/05_AHRQ_factsheet.pdf.

Pham, Hoangmai H., Kelly J. Devers, Sylvia Kuo, and Robert Berenson. 2005. "Health Care Market Trends and the Evolution of Hospitalist Use and Roles." *Journal of General Internal Medicine* 20 (2): 101–7.

Pistoria, Michael J., Alpesh N. Amin, Daniel D. Dressler, Sylvia C. W. McKean, and Tina L. Budnitz. 2006. *The Core Competencies in Hospital Medicine: A Framework for Curriculum Development by the Society of Hospital Medicine.* New York: Wiley-Blackwell.

Pons, P. T., and V. J. Markovchick. 2002. "Eight Minutes or Less: Does the Ambulance Response Time Guideline Impact Trauma Patient Outcome?" *Journal of Emergency Medicine* 23 (1): 43–48. Available at http://www.ingentaconnect.com/content/els/07364679/2002/00000023/00000001/art00460;jsessionid=1c7uhf68322kj.alexandra. doi:10.1016/S0736–4679(02)00460–2.

President's Advisory Commission on Consumer Protection and Quality in the Health Care Industry. 1998. *Advisory Commission's Final Report.* Agency for Healthcare Research and Quality. Available at http://archive.ahrq.gov/hcqual/.

Prevention Quality Indicators Overview. 2004. AHRQ Quality Indicators. Rockville, MD. Agency for Healthcare Research and Quality. Available at http://www.qualityindicators.ahrq.gov/modules/pqi_overview.aspx.

PRNewswire. 2009. "National Association of Healthcare Advocacy Consultants (NAHAC) Launched." *Bio-Medicine.org*, July 30. Available at http://www.bio-medicine.org/medicine-news-1/National-Association-of-Healthcare-Advocacy-Consultants—28NAHAC-29-Launched-53197–1/.

Redhead, C. S. 2003. *Patient Safety: Legislation to Promote Voluntary Reporting of Medical Errors.* CRS Report for Congress. Washington, DC: Congressional Research Service.

Reinhardt, U. E. 2006. "The Pricing of U.S. Hospital Services: Chaos behind a Veil of Secrecy." *Health Affairs* 25 (1): 57–69.

Rich, D. S. 2004. "New JCAHO Medication Management Standards for 2004." *American Society of Health-System Pharmacists* 61 (1): 1349–58.

Robinson, A. R. 2002. "Physician and Public Opinion on Quality of Health Care and the Problem of Medical Errors." *Archives of Internal Medicine* 162: 2186–90.

Rogers, Paul G. 1986. "Milestones in Public Interest Advocacy." In *Advocacy in Health Care: The Power of a Silent Constituency,* ed. Joan Marks, 1–7. Clifton, NJ: Humana Press.

Roscoe, L. A., and T. J. Krizek. 2002. "Reporting Medical Errors: Variables in the System Shape Attitudes toward Reporting Adverse Events." *Bulletin of the American College of Surgeons* 87 (9): 12–17.

Rosenberg, A. L., T. P. Hofer, C. Strachan, C. M. Watts, and R. A. Hayward. 2003. "Accepting Critically Ill Transfer Patients: Adverse Effects on a Referral Center's Outcome and Benchmark Measures." *Annals of Internal Medicine* 138: 882–90.

Rosenthal, J. 2003. *How States Report Errors to the Public: Issues and Barriers.* Portland, ME: National Academy for State Health Policy.

Rosenthal, Jill, Trish Riley, and Maureen Booth. 2000. *State Reporting of Medical Errors and Adverse Events: Results of a 50-State Survey.* Portland, ME: National Academy for State Health Policy.

Rural Task Force of the Governor's EMS & Trauma Advisory Council. 2013. *Texas Elected Officials Guide to Emergency Medical Services.* Available at http://www.nwems.org/Texas%20Elected%20Officials%20Guide%20to%20EMS.pdf.

Sage, W. 2003a. "Medical Liability and Patient Safety." *Health Affairs* 22 (4): 26–36.

———. 2003b. "Understanding the First Malpractice Crisis of the 21st Century." In *Health Law Handbook,* ed. Alice Gosfield. Westlaw. Available at http://ssrn.com/abstract=477100.

Shojania, K. G., J. Showstack, and R. M. Wachter. 2001. "Assessing Hospital Quality: A Review for Clinicians." *Effective Clinical Practice* 4:82–90.

Siegel, D. 2002. "Is There a Hospitalist in the House?" *Outlook* (Fall). St. Louis: Washington University School of Medicine, Office of Medical Public Affairs.

Silverman, R. A., S. Galea, S. Blaney, J. Freese, D. J. Prezant, R. Park, R. Pahk, D. Caron, S. Yoon, J. Epstein, and N. J. Richmond. 2007. "The 'Vertical Response Time': Barriers to Ambulance Response in an Urban Area." *Academic Emergency Medicine* 14 (9): 772–78. Available at http://www3.interscience.wiley.com/journal/119819559/abstract. doi:10.1197/j.aem.2007.04.016. PMID 17601996.

Silverstein, G. 1997. "Physicians' Perceptions of Commercial and Medicaid Managed Care Plans: A Comparison." *Journal of Health Politics, Policy and Law* 22 (1): 5–21.

Sox, H. C. 1999. "The Hospitalist Model: Perspectives of the Patient, the Internist, and Internal Medicine." *Annals of Internal Medicine* 130: 368–72.

Stalhandske, E., J. P. Bagian, and J. Gosbee. 2002. "Department of Veterans Affairs Patient Safety Program." *American Journal of Infection Control* 30 (5): 296–302.

SteelFisher, Gillian K. 2005. *International Innovations in Health Care: Quality Improvement in the UK.* New York: Commonwealth Fund.

Strouse, Richard, Frank Potter, Terisa Davis, John Hall, Stephen Williams, Ellen Herbold, Judy Walsh, Ellyn Boukus, and Jim Reschovsky. 2009. *HSC 2008 Health Tracking Physician Survey Methodology Report.* Technical Publication No. 77. Washington, DC: Center for Studying Health System Change.

Tang, S., B. K. Yudkowsky, and J. Davis. 2003. "Medicaid Participation by Private and Safety Net Pediatricians, 1993 and 2000." *Pediatrics* 112 (2): 368–72.

Teich, J. K., P. R. Merchia, J. L. Schmiz, G. J. Kuperman, C. D. Spurr, and D. W. Bates. 2000. "Effects of Computerized Physician Order Entry on Prescribing Practices." *Archives of Internal Medicine* 160: 2741–47.

"30 Safe Practices for Better Health Care." 2005. AHRQ Fact Sheet. Available at http://www.ahrq.gov/research/findings/factsheets/errors-safety/30safe/index.html.

Thomas, E. J., D. M. Studdert, H. R. Burstin, E. J. Orav, T. Zeena, E. J. Williams, K. M. Howard, P. C. Weiler, and T. A. Brennan. 2000. *Incidence and Types of Adverse Events and Negligent Care in Utah and Colorado. Medical Care* 38 (3): 261–71.

US Congress. 2013. *Compilation of the Social Security Laws.* §1877 of the Social Security Act. 42 C.F.R. §411.350 through §411.389. Available at http://www.ssa.gov/OP_Home/ssact/title18/1877.htm.

US Department of Labor. 2012. *Occupational Outlook Handbook: Healthcare Occupations.* Available at http://www.bls.gov/ooh/healthcare/home.htm.

US Department of Labor, Bureau of Labor Statistics. 2009. "CPI Inflation Calculator." Available at www.bls.gov/data/inflation_calculator.htm.

US Food and Drug Administration. 2013. "Inside Clinical Trials: Testing Medical Products in People." Available at http://www.fda.gov/Drugs/ResourcesForYou/Consumers/ucm143531.htm.

US General Accounting Office. 2002. Report to Chairman, Subcommittee on Defense, Committee on Appropriations, U.S. Senate. *VA and Defense Health Care: Increased Risk of Medication Errors for Shared Patients.* GAO-02-1017. Available at http://www.gao.gov/assets/240/235801.html.

Vasilevskis, E. E., J. Knebel, R. M. Wachter, and A. D. Auerbach. 2007. *The Rise of the Hospitalist in California.* Oakland: California Health Care Foundation.

Vernick, R., and M. Wilson. 2005. "The Rise of Hospitalists, Part 1." *Hospitals and Health Networks* magazine, August. Available at http://www.hhnmag.com/hhnmag/jsp/articledisplay.jsp?dcrpath=HHNMAG/PubsNewsArticle/data/050823HHN_Online_Vernick&domain=HHNMAG.

Wachter, R. M. 2004. "The End of the Beginning: Patient Safety Five Years after *To Err Is Human." Health Affairs (Millwood)* (July–December). Web exclusive. Available at http://www.ncbi.nlm.nih.gov/pubmed/15572380.

———. 2008. "The State of Hospital Medicine in 2008." *Medical Clinics of North America* 92 (2): 265–73.

Wachter, R. M., and L. Goldman. 1996. "The Emerging Role of 'Hospitalists' in the American Healthcare System." *New England Journal of Medicine* 335: 514–17.

———. 2002. "The Hospitalist Movement 5 Years Later." *JAMA* 287:487–94.

Wassernaar, J. D., and S. L. Thran. 2003. *Physician Socioeconomic Statistics.* Chicago: American Medical Association.

Wennberg, J. E., E. S. Fisher, and J. S. Skinner. 2002. "Geography and the Debate over Medicare Reform." *Health Affairs* (July–December): W96–W114.

White, C. 2008. "The Hospital Medicine Movement." *Virtual Mentor* 10 (12): 001–4. Available at http://virtualmentor.ama-assn.org/2008/12/jdsc1-0812.html.

Will, H., and K. O. Jones. 2006. "An Overview of Collegiate Emergency Medical Services." *collegehealth-e* 3 (June–July): 13–14.

Williams, L. K., M. Pladevall, A. M. Fendrick, J. E. Lafata, and L. F. McMahon. 2003. "Differences in the Reporting of Care-Related Patient Injuries to Existing Reporting Systems." *Joint Commission Journal on Quality and Safety* 29: 460–67.

Zarowitz, B., V. Sahney, and L. Savitz. 2003. *The Business Case for Pharmaceutical Management: A Case Study of Henry Ford Health System.* New York: Commonwealth Fund.

Zuckerman, S., A. F. Williams, and K. E. Stockley. 2009. "Trends in Medicaid Physician Fees, 2003–2008." *Health Affairs (Millwood)* 28 (3): w510–w519.

Websites

Acadian (ambulance company): http://www.acadian.com/

AHRQ Fact Sheets: http://www.ahrq.gov/research/findings/factsheets/errors-safety/index.html

AHRQ Patient Safety Indicators, Patient Safety Network: http://psnet.ahrq.gov/resource.aspx?resourceID=1040

AirLife Denver: http://www.airlifedenver.com/

American Medical Response: http://www.amr.net/

Centers for Medicare and Medicaid Services (CMS), Hospital Quality Initiative: http://www.cms.gov/Medicare/Quality-Initiatives-Patient-Assessment-Instruments/HospitalQualityInits/index.html

County of Los Angeles Fire Department: http://www.fire.lacounty.gov/EMS/EMS.asp

Department of Community Health Policies and Procedures (EMS; Fresno/Kings/Madera, California): http://www.co.fresno.ca.us/uploadedFiles/Departments/Public_Health/Divisions/EMS/content/Policies,_Procedures_and_Memos/content/Fresno,_Kings_and_Madera_Counties/001_-_099/021.pdf

FDNYEMS (Fire Department, New York City): http://fdnyems.com/

Flight for Life Colorado: http://www.flightforlifecolorado.org/

Guardian Ambulance Service (Los Angeles): http://www.guardianambulance.org/ver_1.html

Institute for Healthcare Improvement: http://www.ihi.org/IHI/Programs/Campaign/

Institute of Medicine of the National Academies: http://www.iom.edu

Joint Commission Quality Check (quality reports for Joint Commission–certified disease-specific care programs): www.qualitycheck.org

Maryland State Police Aviation Command: http://www.mspaviation.org/frames.asp

Massachusetts Coalition for the Prevention of Medical Errors: http://www.macoalition.org/

Medical Response Emergency Software (MRES): http://www.mresnet.com/mresscreenshots.asp

Monroe Volunteer EMS (New York): http://www.monroeems.org/

National Registry of Emergency Medical Technicians (NREMT): http://www.nremt.org/about/nremt_news.asp

Rural/Metro Corporation (private fire protection and ambulance services): http://www.ruralmetro.com/

Texas A&M University, Texas Engineering Extension Service, Emergency Services Training Institute: http://www.teex.org/esti/

Upton Fire & EMS Department (Massachusetts): http://www.upton.ma.us/Pages/UptonMA_FireEMS/index

US General Services Administration: http://www.gsa.gov

US Parks Police (Aviation Unit): http://www.nps.gov/uspp/avipag.htm

Your Medicare coverage: Ambulance Services: http://www.medicare.gov/coverage/ambulance-services.html

INDEX

Pediatric Advanced Life Support (PALS), 84
pelvis fractures, 73
Penn, William, 14
"personally operated vehicles" (POVs), 60, 64
Pfizer, 117
pharmaceutical and biotechnology companies, 117–18, *176–77*
Pharmaceutical Research and Manufacturers of America, 178
pharmacists and pharmacy services, 120, 126–28, *176–77*
phones and emergencies, *56*
physical exams, 15, 21–22
physical therapy, 114–15
physician assistants (PAs), 35–38, *45*
physicians, 28–31
    advocacy by, 195–96, 197, 199
    and changes in the field, 196–97
    credentials of, *45*
    earliest physicians, 12
    as employees, 197, 198–99
    fake doctors, 166
    in medical director role, *53*
    patient's relationship with, 195–96
population density, *70*
post-anesthesia care unit (PACU), 107
postoperative admissions, 95–98
power of access or attorney, 93–94
preexisting conditions, 180
premiums, 178
prescriptions, 119–26, *121*, 127–28. *See also* medications
primary care physicians, 15–16, 97–98
primogeniture, 11–12
prior authorizations, 181
privacy protection, 194–95
private emergency services, 58–59, 66
progressive disease evaluation errors, 169
public health policies, 175–76

randomization, 150
rates for medical services, 189
redness at wound site, 113
regional anesthesia, 100
registered nurses (RNs), 41, *45*
religion and ancient healing practices, 9–13

resting after surgeries, 108–9
Rome, ancient, 10–11

Sanofi, 117
scheduled drugs, 124–25
Science Daily, 117
secular authorities and hospitals, 13
sedation, 100–101
sexual dysfunction, 134
showering, 110
Shriners Hospitals for Children, 65
side effects, 150–51
signage, 60, *61*, 164, 170
signs, symptoms compared to, 22
single-blinded trials, 150
Sisters of St. Joseph, 14
sleep medications, 109
slurred speech, 79
smoking, 106
SOAP notes, 17–25, *24*
    assessment section, 22–23
    objective section, 21–22
    plan section, 23–25
    subjective section, 17–21
specialists and specialization, 16, 31–32, *33–34*
speech, changes in, 79, 135
spine trauma, 73
St. John's Ambulance Corps, 12
stroke care, 71, 78–83
subdural hematomas, 76
surgeries and surgeons, 89–115
    and advocates, 95
    anesthesia for, 98–102
    and communication, 92–93
    credentials of surgeons, 46
    day surgery vs. postoperative admission, 95–98
    and hygiene, 107, 110–11
    mental functioning after, *112*
    mistakes made in, 164, 165
    multiple procedures, 103
    packing for, 106–7
    and post-anesthesia care unit (PACU), 107
    and post-op recovery, 107–8, 112–15
    preparing for, 93
    questions to ask, 96–98
    researching, 96